Praise for Michael E. Gerber, Dr. Alan Kwong Hing, Christopher Barrow, and *The E-Myth Dentist*

I was first introduced to *The E-Myth Revisited* by my business coach, Chris Barrow, 6 years ago. It became the cornerstone of my business development. I have continued to work closely with Chris and, for the last 12 months, with Dr. Al Kwong Hing. **Their wealth of knowledge within the sector and the authenticity they bring to this project means *The E-Myth Dentist* is a must read for anyone wanting to grow their dental business and be the best they can be.**

Dr. Alex Jones BSc (Hons), BDS

This book is not to be missed. Michael E. Gerber has partnered with Chris Barrow and Dr. Al Kwong Hing to provide an invaluable business resource. **A winner for everyone in the rapidly changing world of dentistry today.**

Dr. Andrew Fennell BDS (Lond)

***The E-Myth Dentist* is a must-read for any dentist who owns his own business.** It closes that gap that dental school left us with, as we had no exposure to business training. It provides you with all the necessary tools for success and balancing work with life. It gives refreshing, ethical, and relevant advice, which is generously shared by Michael Gerber, Chris Barrow, and Dr. Al Kwong Hing. Highly recommend.

Dr. Abeer Al-Adhami BDS

I have always loved being a dentist, but not so much a business owner! I bought *The E-Myth Dentist* and read it from cover to cover in three days. I literally could not put this book down! **The E-Myth Dentist was an exciting read and gave me so many insights to transform my practice. It has ignited my passion for my business again!** Every practicing dentist needs to read this book.

Dr. Stacey Doncaster DDS BSc

In dental school, we learn the basics of dentistry while barely scratching the surface on how to run a business. I have come to learn that being a business owner is far more complex than dentistry itself. **One of the great strengths of *The E-Myth Dentist* is how it simplifies what seem to be very complex issues.** I highly recommend this book!

Dr. Caleb Porter DDS

I first read *The E-Myth* by Michael Gerber over 10 years ago. I was then fortunate enough to see him present alongside Chris Barrow in 2005. They have both had a profound influence on my life as a practitioner and business owner. Add in to the mix Canadian dentist and entrepreneur Dr. Al Kwong-Hing and you have a formidable powerhouse of business knowledge. **The E- Myth Dentist brings together the vast experience of these three entrepreneurs and will change the way you approach your dental practice, forever.** Time to start working ON the business not IN the business!

Dr. Andrew Legg BDS, MFDS RCS Ed

Michael Gerber's *The E-Myth* is one of only four books I recommend as required reading. **For those looking to start and build a business of their own, this is the man who has coached more successful entrepreneurs than the next ten gurus combined.**

Timothy Ferris, #1 *New York Times* best-selling author, *The 4-Hour Workweek*

Everyone needs a mentor, someone who tells it like it is, holds you accountable, and shows you your good, bad, and ugly. For millions of small-business owners, Michael Gerber is that person. Let Michael be your mentor and you are in for a kick in the pants, the ride of a lifetime.

John Jantsch, author, *Duct Tape Marketing*

Michael Gerber's strategies in *The E-Myth* were instrumental in building my company from two employees to a global organization; I can't wait to see how applying the strategies from *Awakening the Entrepreneur Within* will affect its growth!

Dr. Ivan Misner, founder and chairman, BNI; author, *Masters of Sales*

Michael Gerber's gift to isolate the issues and present simple, direct, business-changing solutions shines bright with *Awakening the Entrepreneur Within*. If you're interested in developing an entrepreneurial vision and plan that inspires others to action, buy this book, read it, and apply the processes Gerber brilliantly defines.

Tim Templeton, author, *The Referral of a Lifetime*

Michael Gerber is a master instructor and a leader's leader. As a combat F-15 fighter pilot, I had to navigate complex missions with life-and-death consequences, but until I read *The E-Myth* and met Michael Gerber, my transition to the world of small business was a nightmare with no real flight plan. The hands-on, practical magic of Michael's turnkey systems magnified by the raw power of his keen insight and wisdom have changed my life forever.

Steve Olds, CEO, Stratworx.com

Michael Gerber truly, truly understands what it takes to be a successful practicing entrepreneur and business owner. He has demonstrated to me over six years of working with him that for those who stay the course and learn much more than just "how to work on their business and not in it," then they will reap rich rewards. I finally franchised my business, and the key to unlocking this kind of potential in any business is the teaching of Michael's work.

Chris Owen, marketing director, Royal Armouries (International) PLC

Because of Michael Gerber, I transformed my twenty-four-hour-a-day, seven-day-a-week job (also called a small business) into a multimillion-dollar turnkey business. This in turn set the foundation for my worldwide training firm. I am living my dream because of Michael Gerber.

Howard Partridge, Phenomenal Products Inc

Michael's work has been an inspiration to us. **His books have helped us get free from the out-of-control life that we once had. His no-nonsense approach kept us focused on our ultimate aim rather than day-to-day stresses. He has helped take our business to levels we couldn't have imagined possible.** In the Dreaming Room™ made us totally re-evaluate how we thought about our business and our life. We have now redesigned our life so we can manifest the dreams we unearthed in Michael's Dreaming Room™.

Jo and Steve Davison, founders, The Spinal Health Clinic
Chiropractic Group and www.your-dream-life.com .

Michael Gerber is an outrageous revolutionary who is changing the way the world does business. **He dares you to commit to your grandest dreams and then shows you how to make the impossible a reality. If you let him, this man will change your life.**

Fiona Fallon, founder, Divine and The Bottom Line

Michael Gerber is a genius. Every successful business person I meet has read Michael Gerber, refers to Michael Gerber, and lives by his words. You just can't get enough of Michael Gerber. **He has the innate (and rare) ability to tap into one's soul, look deeply, and tell you what you need to hear. And then, he inspires you and equips you with the tools to get it done.**

Pauline O'Malley, CEO, TheRevenueBuilder

When asked "Who was the most influential person in your life?" I am one of the thousands who don't hesitate to say "Michael E. Gerber." **Michael helped transform me from someone dreaming of retirement to someone dreaming of working until age one hundred.** This awakening is the predictable outcome of anyone reading Michael's new book.

Thomas O. Bardeen

Michael Gerber is an incredible business philosopher, guru, perhaps even a seer. He has an amazing intuition, which allows him to see in an instant what everybody else is missing; he sees opportunity everywhere. **While I was in the Dreaming Room™, Michael gave me the gift of seeing through the eyes of an awakened entrepreneur, and instantly my business changed from a regional success to serving clients on four continents.**

Keith G. Schiehl, president, Rent-a-Geek Computer Services

Michael Gerber forced me to think big, think real, and gave me the support network to make it happen. A new wave of entrepreneurs is rising, much in thanks to his amazing efforts and very practical approach to doing business.

Christian Kessner, founder, Higher Ground Retreats and Events

Michael Gerber is among the very few who truly understand entrepreneurship and small business. While others talk about these topics in the form of theories, methodologies, processes, and so on, Michael goes to the heart of the issues. **Whenever Michael writes about entrepreneurship, soak it in, as it is not only good for your business, but great for your soul.** His words will help you to keep your passion and balance while sailing through the uncertain sea of entrepreneurship.

Raymond Yeh, co-author, *The Art of Business*

Michael's understanding of entrepreneurship and small-business management has been a difference maker for countless businesses, including Infusion Software. **His insights into the entrepreneurial process of building a business are a must-read for every small-business owner.** The vision, clarity, and leadership that came out of our Dreaming Room™ experience were just what our company needed to recognize our potential and motivate the whole company to achieve it.

Clate Mask, president and CEO, Infusion Software

Michael Gerber is a truly remarkable man. His steady openness of mind and ability to get to the deeper level continue to be an inspiration and encouragement to me. **He seems to always ask that one question that forces the new perspective to break open, and he approaches the new coming method in a fearless way.**

Rabbi Levi Cunin, Chabad of Malibu

The Dreaming Room™ experience was literally life-changing for us. **Within months, we were able to start our foundation and make several television appearances owing to his teachings.** He has an incredible charisma, which is priceless, but above all Michael Gerber awakens passion from within, enabling you to take action with dramatic results . . . starting today!

Shona and Shaun Carcary
Trinity Property Investments Inc. — Home Vestors franchises

I thought *E-Myth* was an awkward name! What could this book do for me? **But when I finally got to reading it . . . it was what I was looking for all along.** Then, to top it off, I took a twenty-seven-hour trip to San Diego just to attend the Dreaming Room™, where Michael touched my heart, my mind, and my soul.

Helmi Natto, president, Eye 2 Eye Optics, Saudi Arabia

I attended In the Dreaming Room™ and was challenged by Michael Gerber to "Go out and do what's impossible." So I did; **I became an author and international speaker and used Michael's principles to create a world-class company that will change and save lives all over the world.**

Dr. Don Kennedy, MBA; author, *5 AM & Already Behind*, www.bahbits.com

I went to the Dreaming Room™ to have Michael Gerber fix my business. He talked about Dreaming. What was this Dreaming? I was too busy working! Too busy being miserable, angry, frustrated, behind in what I was trying to accomplish. And losing everything I was working for. **Then Michael Gerber woke up the dreamer in me and remade my life and my business.**

Pat Doorn, president, Mountain View Electric Ltd.

Michael Gerber can captivate a room full of entrepreneurs and take them to a place where they can focus on the essentials that are the underpinning of every successful business. He gently leads them from where they are to where they need to be in order to change the world.

Francine Hardaway, CEO, Stealthmode Partners
founder, the Arizona Entrepreneurship Conferences

The E Myth
Dentist

*Why Most Dental
Practices Don't Work
and What to Do About It*

MICHAEL E. GERBER

DR. ALAN KWONG HING
CHRISTOPHER BARROW

PRODIGY
BUSINESS BOOKS

Published by
Prodigy Business Books, Inc., Carlsbad, California.

Production Team
Patricia Beaulieu, COO, Prodigy Business Books, Inc.; Jenny Sommerfeld, editor; Erich Broesel, cover designer, BroeselDesign, Inc.; Nancy Ratkiewich, book production, njr productions; Jeff Kassebaum, Michael E. Gerber author photographer, Jeff Kassebaum and Co.; Kortney Kwong Hing, Dr. Alan Kwong Hing co-author photographer; Stuart Reekie, Christopher Barrow co-author photographer

For general information on other products and services, please visit the website: www.michaelegerber.com.

ISBN 978-1-61835-025-1 (cloth)
ISBN 978-1-61835-026-8 (audio)
ISBN 978-1-61835-027-5 (e-book)

Printed in the United States of America

10 9 8 7 6 5 4 3 2 1

To Luz Delia, whose heart expands mine,
whose soul inspires mine,
whose boldness reaches for the stars, thank you,
forever, for being, truly mine . . .

—Michael E. Gerber

CONTENTS

i

A WORD ABOUT THIS BOOK

Michael E. Gerber

My first E-Myth book was published in 1985. It was called *The E-Myth: Why Most Businesses Don't Work and What to Do About It*. Since that book, and the company I created to provide business development services to its many readers, millions have read *The E-Myth* and the book that followed it, called *The E-Myth Revisited*, and tens of thousands have participated in our E-Myth Mastery programs.

The co-authors of this book, Dr. Alan Kwong Hing and Christopher Barrow, are two of my more enthusiastic readers, and as a direct result of their enthusiasm, their practice became one of those clients. They became, over the years, my friends.

This book is two things: the product of my lifelong work conceiving, developing, and growing the E-Myth way into a business model that has been applied to every imaginable kind of company in the world, as well as a product of Al and Chris' extraordinary experience and success applying the E-Myth to their businesses.

So it was that one day, while sitting with my muse, which I think of as my inner voice, and which many who know me think of as "here he goes again!" I thought about the creation of an entire series of E-Myth Expert books. That series, including this book, would be co-authored by experts in every industry who had successfully applied my E-Myth principles to the extreme development of a practice—a very small company—with the intent of growing it nationwide, and even worldwide, which is what Al and Chris had in mind as they began to discover the almost infinite range of opportunities provided by thinking the E-Myth way.

Upon seeing the possibilities of this new idea, I immediately invited co-authors such as Al and Chris to join me. They said, "Let's do it!" and so we did.

Welcome to *The E-Myth Dentist: Why Most Dental Practices Don't Work and What to Do About It.*

Read it, enjoy it, and let us—Al, Chris, and I—help you apply the E-Myth to the re-creation, development, and extreme growth of your dental practice into an enterprise that you can be justifiably proud of.

To your life, your wisdom, and the life and success of your clients, I wish you good reading.

—Michael E. Gerber
Co-Founder/Chairman
Michael E. Gerber Companies, Inc.
Carlsbad, California
www.michaelegerber.com/co-author

A NOTE FROM AL AND CHRIS

Dr. Alan Kwong Hing
Christopher Barrow

We remember well the first time we each read Michael Gerber's *The E-Myth: Why Most Businesses Don't Work and What to Do About It*. Just like hundreds of thousands of readers over the years, we both found ourselves thinking, "This is me!"

Quite simply, Michael's E-Myth philosophy connected with us in a way unlike any business book had done before, or has done since. It put our business lives in perspective and engaged with us in a way so few books are able. That's because at its core, *The E-Myth* isn't a book about theory or practicalities, but about people. And that is the magic of E-Myth.

Like an ancient prophet, Michael Gerber told a story about a person who had a very real and authentic human experience. Every aspect of the pain of business ownership resonated with us. And that's why the book has become an international bestseller that's stood the test of time—because it resonates.

Given just how important the E-Myth is to both our lives, when the opportunity came up to work on *The E-Myth Dentist*, we really couldn't say no! Still to this day, one of the first things either of us ask when we meet people looking for advice is, "Have you read Gerber?" That's because Michael Gerber's E-Myth philosophy is now written in stone in terms of the way in which we interact with our clients, and is fundamental to how any good successful dental practice should operate.

These are exciting times to be involved with dentistry. For ourselves, personally, we are both involved with exciting new projects. It's ironic that in the twenty or so years since we first discovered E-Myth, Michael's fantastic book has become more relevant than in any other time in that period. We have a lot of hopes and aspirations for our businesses, and one of our hopes is that we might each be able to say, "That was an E-Myth business."

Now, by working with Michael on *The E-Myth Dentist*, we hope that we can share our insight into the amazing world of E-Myth dentistry so you, too, can read this book and think, "Wow, this is me!" We know it changed our lives when we first discovered the E-Myth way of thinking, and now with *The E-Myth Dentist*, we hope it will change yours, too.

—Dr. Alan Kwong Hing, DDS MSc
Founder/CEO Maritime Dental Group
Ontario and Atlantic Canada
www.maritimedentalgroup.ca

—Christopher Barrow
Partner
7Connections
Manchester, England
www.7connections.com

PREFACE

Michael E. Gerber

I am not a dentist, though I have helped dozens of dentists reinvent their practices over the past thirty-five years.

I like to think of myself as a thinker, maybe even a dreamer. Yes, I like to *do* things. But before I jump in and get my hands dirty, I prefer to think through what I'm going to do and figure out the best way to do it. I imagine the impossible, dream big, and then try to figure out how the impossible can become the possible. After that, it's about how to turn the possible into reality.

Over the years, I've made it my business to study how things work and how people work—specifically, how things and people work best together to produce optimum results. That means creating an organization that can do great things and achieve more than any other organization can.

This book is about how to produce the best results as a real-world dentist in the development, expansion, and *liberation* of your practice. In the process, you will come to understand what the practice of dentistry—as a *business*—is, and what it isn't. If you keep focusing on what it isn't, you're destined for failure. But if you turn your sights on what it *is*, the tide will turn.

This book, intentionally small, is about big ideas. The topics we'll be discussing in this book are the very issues that dentists face daily in their practice. You know what they are: money, management, patients, and many more. My aim is to help you begin the exciting process of totally transforming the way you do business. As such, I'm confident that *The E-Myth Dentist* could well be the most important book on the practice of dentistry as a business that you'll ever read.

Unlike other books on the market, my goal is not to tell you how to do the work you do. Instead, I want to share with you the E-Myth philosophy as a way to revolutionize the way you think about the work you do. I'm convinced that this new way of thinking is something dentists everywhere must adopt in order for their dental practice to flourish during these trying times. I call it strategic thinking, as opposed to tactical thinking.

In strategic thinking, also called systems thinking, you, the dentist, will begin to think about your entire practice—the broad scope of it—instead of focusing on its individual parts. You will begin to see the end game (perhaps for the first time) rather than just the day-to-day routine that's consuming you—the endless, draining work I call "doing it, doing it, doing it."

Understanding strategic thinking will enable you to create a practice that becomes a successful business, with the potential to flourish as an even more successful enterprise. But in order for you to accomplish this, your practice, your business, and certainly your enterprise must work *apart* from you instead of *because* of you.

The E-Myth philosophy says that a highly successful dental practice can grow into a highly successful dental business, which in turn can become the foundation for an inordinately successful dental enterprise that runs smoothly and efficiently *without* the dentist having to be in the office for ten hours a day, six days a week.

So what is "The E-Myth," exactly? The E-Myth is short for the Entrepreneurial Myth, which says that most businesses fail to fulfill their potential because most people starting their own business are not entrepreneurs at all. They're actually what I call technicians suffering from an entrepreneurial seizure. When *technicians suffering from an entrepreneurial seizure* start a dental practice of their own, they almost always end up working themselves into a frenzy; their days are booked solid with appointments, one patient after another. These dentists are burning the candle at both ends, fueled by too much coffee and too little sleep, and most of the time, they can't even stop to think.

In short, the E-Myth says that most dentists don't own a true business—most own a job. They're doing it, doing it, doing it, hoping like hell to get some time off, but never figuring out how to get their business to run without them. And if your business doesn't run well without you, what happens when you can't be in two places at once? Ultimately, your practice will fail.

There are a number of prestigious schools throughout the world dedicated to teaching the science of dentistry. The problem is they fail to teach the *business* of it. And because no one is being taught how to run a practice as a business, some dentists find themselves having to close their doors every year. You could be a world-class expert in orthodontics or oral surgery, but when it comes to building a successful business all that specified knowledge matters exactly zilch.

The good news is that you don't have to be among the statistics of failure in the dental profession. The E-Myth philosophy I am about to share with you in this book has been successfully applied to thousands of dental practices just like yours with extraordinary results.

The key to transforming your practice—and your life—is to grasp the profound difference between going to work *on* your practice (systems thinker) and going to work *in* your practice (tactical thinker). In other words, it's the difference between going to work on your practice as an entrepreneur and going to work in your practice as a dentist.

The two are not mutually exclusive. In fact, they are essential to each other. The problem with most dental practices is that the systems thinker—the entrepreneur—is completely absent. And so is the vision.

The E-Myth philosophy says that the key to transforming your practice into a successful enterprise is knowing how to transform yourself from successful dental technician into successful technician-manager-entrepreneur. In the process, everything you do in your dental practice will be transformed. The door is then open to turning it into the kind of practice it should be—a practice, a business, an enterprise of pure joy.

The E-Myth not only *can* work for you, it *will* work for you. In the process, it will give you an entirely new experience of your business and beyond.

To your future and your life. Good reading.

—Michael E. Gerber
Co-Founder/Chairman
Michael E. Gerber Companies, Inc.
Carlsbad, California
www.michaelegerber.com/co-author

ACKNOWLEDGMENTS

Michael E. Gerber

As always, and never to be forgotten, there are those who give of themselves to make my work possible.

To my dearest and most forgiving partner, wife, friend, and co-founder, Luz Delia Gerber, whose love and commitment takes me to places I would often not go unaccompanied. .

To Jenny Sommerfeld whose keen editorial eye helped to polish the final package.

Erich Broesel, our stand-alone graphic designer and otherwise visual genius who supported the creation of all things visual that will forever be all things Gerber, we thank you, deeply, for your continuous contribution of things both temporal and eternal.

To Trish Beaulieu, wow, you are splendid.

And to Nancy Ratkiewich, whose work has been essential for you who are reading this.

To those many, many dreamers, thinkers, storytellers, and leaders, whose travels with me in The Dreaming Room™ have given me life, breath, and pleasure unanticipated before we met. To those many participants in my life (you know who you are), thank you for taking me seriously, and joining me in this exhilarating quest.

And, of course, to my co-authors, all of you, your genius, wisdom, intelligence, and wit have supplied me with a grand view of the world, which would never have been the same without you.

Love to all.

ACKNOWLEDGMENTS

Dr. Alan Kwong Hing

In writing this book, I have gone through a process of self-discovery to review the journey that I have undertaken to get me where I am today and where I will go tomorrow. My journey could not have been possible without the support, advice, encouragement, feedback and advocacy of my wife, Brenda. We have been together since our teenage years—a rare thing itself these days—and by embracing open and honest lines of communication, we have endured. We have always encouraged each other to define our own positions in the world and encouraged each other 100% to do it and not think it. My two daughters, Kortney and Kailyn, are my inspiration to live life large as a citizen of the world, but in a humble and grounded way.

ACKNOWLEDGMENTS

Christopher Barrow

To my wonderful and unconditionally loving partner, Anneliese. To my best friends, the five Barrow kids—Jon, Alex, Josh, Rachel and Ellie.

To my traveling companions on this wonderful adventure. To my coaching clients over 20 years—the best R&D team ever!

To all the trainers, consultants, coaches, speakers, and authors who have shared their wisdom with me over the years.

To my friends in UK and Irish dentistry.

And a special thanks to Michael Gerber for the moment when he touched my spirit on the subject of business and then engaged my mind and body in the pursuit of excellence.

INTRODUCTION

Michael E. Gerber

A s I write this book, the recession continues to take its toll on American businesses. Like any other industry, dentistry is not immune. Dentists all over the country are watching as patients defer visits for checkups and wellness care. At a time when per capita disposable income is at an all-time low, many people are choosing not to spend their hard-earned money on dental services for themselves and even for their children. As a result, dental care moves from the realm of necessity to luxury, and regrettably, healthy lifestyles and preventive care become an expendable concern while industry revenue takes a sizable dip into the red.

Faced with a struggling economy and fewer and fewer patients, many dentists I've met are asking themselves, "Why did I ever become a dentist in the first place?"

And it isn't just a money problem. After thirty-five years of working with small businesses, many of them dental practices, I'm convinced that the dissatisfaction experienced by countless dentists is not just about money. To be frank, the recession doesn't deserve all the blame, either. While the financial crisis our country is facing certainly hasn't made things any better, the problem started long before the economy tanked. Let's dig a little deeper. Let's go back to school.

Can you remember that far back? Whichever university or college of dentistry you attended, you probably had some great teachers who helped you become the fine Doctor of Dentistry you are. These schools excel at teaching the science of dentistry; they'll teach you everything you need to know about medical physiology, dental anatomy, and oral microbiology. But what they *don't* teach is the consummate skill set needed to be a successful dentist, and they certainly don't teach what it takes to build a successful dental enterprise.

Obviously, something is seriously wrong. The education that dental professionals receive in school doesn't go far enough, deep enough, broad enough. Colleges of dentistry don't teach you how to relate to the *enterprise* of dentistry or to the *business* of dentistry; they only teach you how to relate to the *practice* of dentistry. In other words, they merely teach you how to be an *effective* rather than a *successful* dentist. Last time I checked, they weren't offering degrees in success. That's why most dentists are effective, but few are successful.

Although a successful dentist must be effective, an effective dentist does not have to be—and in most cases isn't—successful.

An effective dentist is capable of executing his or her duties with as much certainty and professionalism as possible.

A successful dentist, on the other hand, works balanced hours, has little stress, leads rich and rewarding relationships with friends and family, and has an economic life that is diverse, fulfilling, and shows a continuous return on investment.

A successful dentist finds time and ways to give back to the community but at little cost to his or her sense of ease.

A successful dentist is a leader, not simply someone who teaches patients how to care for themselves and protect their oral hygiene, but a sage; a rich person (in the broadest sense of the word); a strong father, mother, wife, or husband; a friend, teacher, mentor, and spiritually grounded human being; and a person who can see clearly into all aspects of what it means to lead a fulfilling life.

So let's go back to the original question. Why did you become a dentist? Were you striving to just be an effective one, or did you dream about real and resounding success?

I don't know how you've answered that question in the past, but I am confident that once you understand the strategic thinking laid out in this book, you will answer it differently in the future.

If the ideas here are going to be of value to you, it's critical that you begin to look at yourself in a different, more productive way. I am suggesting that you go beyond the mere technical aspects of your daily job as a Doctor of Dentistry and begin instead to think strategically about your dental practice as both a business and an enterprise.

I often say that most *practices* don't work—the people who own them do. In other words, most dental practices are jobs for the dentists who own them. Does this sound familiar? The dentist, overcome by an entrepreneurial seizure, has started his or her own practice, become his or her own boss, and now works for a lunatic!

The result: the dentist is running out of time, patience, and ultimately money. Not to mention paying the worst price anyone can pay for the inability to understand what a true practice is, what a true business is, and what a true enterprise is—the price of his or her life.

In this book I'm going to make the case for why you should think differently about what you do and why you do it. It isn't just the future of your dental practice that hangs in the balance. It's the future of your life.

The E-Myth Dentist is an exciting departure from my other sole-authored books. In this book, an expert—a licensed dentist who has successfully applied the E-Myth to the development of his dental practice—is sharing his secrets about how he achieved extraordinary results using the E-Myth paradigm. In addition to the time-tested E-Myth strategies and systems I'll be sharing with you, you'll benefit from the wisdom, guidance, and practical tips provided by a legion of dentists who've been in your shoes.

The problems that afflict dental practices today don't only exist in the field of health care; the same problems are confronting every organization of every size, in every industry in every country in the world. *The E-Myth Dentist* is next in a new series of E-Myth Expert books that will serve as a launching pad for Michael E. Gerber Partners™ to bring a legacy of expertise to small, struggling businesses in *all* industries. This series will offer an exciting opportunity to understand and apply the significance of E-Myth methodology in both theory and practice to businesses in need of development and growth.

The E-Myth says that only by conducting your business in a truly innovative and independent way will you ever realize the unmatched joy that comes from creating a truly independent business, a business that works *without* you rather than *because* of you.

The E-Myth says that it is only by learning the difference between the work of a *business* and the business of *work* that dentists will be freed from the predictable and often overwhelming tyranny of the unprofitable, unproductive routine that consumes them on a daily basis.

The E-Myth says that what will make the ultimate difference between the success or failure of your dental practice is first and foremost how you *think* about your business, as opposed to how hard you work in it.

So, let's think it through together. Let's think about those things—work, patients, money, time—that dominate the world of dentists everywhere.

Let's talk about planning. About growth. About management. About getting a life!

Let's think about improving your and your family's life through the development of an extraordinary practice. About getting the life you've always dreamed of but never thought you could actually have.

Envision the future you want, and the future is yours.

The Story of Steve and Peggy

Michael E. Gerber

You leave home to seek your fortune and, when you get it, you go home and share it with your family.

—Anita Baker

Every business is a family business. To ignore this truth is to court disaster.

This is true whether or not family members actually work in the business. Whatever their relationship with the business, every member of a dentist's family will be greatly affected by the decisions a dentist makes about the business. There's just no way around it.

Unfortunately, like most doctors, dentists tend to compartmentalize their lives. They view their practice as a profession—what they do—and therefore it's none of their family's business.

"This has nothing to do with you," says the dentist to his wife, with blind conviction. "I leave work at the office and family at home."

And with equal conviction, I say, "Not true!"

In actuality, your family and dental practice are inextricably linked to one another. What's happening in your practice is also happening at home. Consider the following and ask yourself if each is true:

- If you're angry at work, you're also angry at home.
- If you're out of control in your dental practice, you're equally out of control at home.
- If you're having trouble with money in your practice, you're also having trouble with money at home.
- If you have communication problems in your practice, you're also having communication problems at home.
- If you don't trust in your practice, you don't trust at home.
- If you're secretive in your practice, you're equally secretive at home.

And you're paying a huge price for it!

The truth is that your practice and your family are one—and you're the link. Or you should be. Because if you try to keep your practice and your family apart, if your practice and your family are strangers, you will effectively create two separate worlds that can never whole-heartedly serve each other. Two worlds that split each other apart.

Let me tell you the story of Steve and Peggy Walsh.

The Walshes met in college. They were lab partners in organic chemistry, Steve a pre-dental student and Peggy pre-nursing. When their lab discussions started to wander beyond spectroscopy and carboxylic acids and into their personal lives, they discovered they had a lot in common. By the end of the course, they weren't just talking in class; they were talking on the phone every night . . . and *not* about organic chemistry.

Steve thought Peggy was absolutely brilliant, and Peggy considered Steve the most passionate man she knew. It wasn't long before they were engaged and planning their future together. A week after graduation, they were married in a lovely garden ceremony in Peggy's childhood home.

While Steve studied at a prestigious college of dentistry, Peggy entered a nursing program nearby. Over the next few years, the couple worked hard to keep their finances afloat. They worked long hours and studied constantly; they were often exhausted and struggled to make ends meet. But through it all, they were committed to what they were doing and to each other.

After passing his state boards, Steve became an associate doctor in a busy practice while Peggy began working in a large hospital nearby. Soon afterward, the couple had their first son, and Peggy decided to take some time off from the hospital to be with him. Those were good years. Steve and Peggy loved each other very much, were active members in their church, participated in community organizations, and spent quality time together. The Walshes considered themselves one of the most fortunate families they knew.

But work became troublesome. Steve grew increasingly frustrated with the way the practice was run. "I want to go into business for myself," he announced one night at the dinner table. "I want to start my own practice."

Steve and Peggy spent many nights talking about the move. Was it something they could afford? Did Steve really have the skills necessary to make a dental practice a success? Were there enough patients to go around? What impact would such a move have on Peggy's career at the local hospital, their lifestyle, their son, their relationship? They asked all the questions they thought they needed to answer before Steve went into business for himself ... but they never really drew up a concrete plan.

Finally, tired of talking and confident that he could handle whatever he might face, Steve committed to starting his own dental practice. Because she loved and supported him, Peggy agreed, offering her own commitment to help in any way she could. So Steve quit his job, took out a second mortgage on their home, and leased a small office nearby.

In the beginning, things went well. A building boom had hit the town, and new families were pouring into the area. Steve had no trouble getting new patients. His practice expanded, quickly outgrowing his office.

Within a year, Steve had employed an office manager, Clarissa, to run the front desk and handle the administrative side of the business.

He also hired a bookkeeper, Tim, to handle the finances. Steve was ecstatic with the progress his young practice had made. He celebrated by taking his wife and son on vacation to Italy.

Of course, managing a business was more complicated and time-consuming than working for someone else. Steve not only supervised all the jobs Clarissa and Tim did, but also was continually looking for work to keep everyone busy. When he wasn't scanning journals of dentistry to stay abreast of what was going on in the field or fulfilling continuing-education requirements to stay current on the standards of care, he was going to the bank, wading through patient paperwork, or speaking with insurance companies (which usually degenerated into *arguing* with insurance companies). He also found himself spending more and more time on the telephone dealing with patient complaints and nurturing relationships.

As the months went by and more and more patients came through the door, Steve had to spend even more time just trying to keep his head above water.

By the end of its second year, the practice, now employing two full-time and two part-time people, had moved to a larger office downtown. The demands on Steve's time had grown with the practice.

He began leaving home earlier in the morning and returning later at night. He drank more. He rarely saw his son anymore. For the most part, Steve was resigned to the problem. He saw the hard work as essential to building the "sweat equity" he had long heard about.

Money was also becoming a problem for Steve. Although the practice was growing like crazy, money always seemed scarce when it was really needed. He had discovered that insurance companies were often slow to pay, and when they did, they cut his fee.

When Steve had worked for somebody else, he had been paid twice a month. In his own practice, he often had to wait—sometimes for months. He was still owed money on billings he had completed more than ninety days before.

When he complained to late-paying insurers, it fell on deaf ears. They would shrug, smile, and promise to do their best to review the claims, adding, "But your care plan does not meet medical necessity according to our guidelines." Of course, no matter how slowly Steve got paid, he still had to pay his people. This became a relentless problem. Steve often felt like a juggler dancing on a tightrope. A fire burned in his stomach day and night.

To make matters worse, Steve began to feel that Peggy was insensitive to his troubles. Not that he often talked to his wife about the practice. "Business is business" was Steve's mantra. "It's my responsibility to handle things at the office and Peggy's responsibility to take care of her own job and the family."

Peggy was working late hours at the hospital, and they'd brought in a nanny to help with their son. Steve couldn't help but notice that his wife seemed resentful, and her apparent lack of understanding baffled him. Didn't she see that he had a practice to take care of? That he was doing it all for his family? Apparently not.

As time went on, Steve became even more consumed and frustrated by his practice. When he went off on his own, he remembered saying, "I don't like people telling me what to do." But people were still telling him what to do. On one particularly frustrating morning, his office had to get an insurance authorization for a $57 intraoral x-ray. It required a long-distance call and twenty-five minutes on hold. Steve was furious.

Not surprisingly, Peggy grew more frustrated by her husband's lack of communication. She cut back on her own hours at the hospital to focus on their family, but her husband still never seemed to be around. Their relationship grew tense and strained. The rare moments they were together were more often than not peppered by long silences—a far cry from the heartfelt conversations that had characterized their relationship's early days, when they'd talk into the wee hours of the morning.

Meanwhile, Tim, the bookkeeper, was also becoming a problem for Steve. Tim never seemed to have the financial information Steve needed to make decisions about payroll, patient billing, and general operating expenses, let alone how much money was available for Steve and Peggy's living expenses.

When questioned, Tim would shift his gaze to his feet and say, "Listen, Steve, I've got a lot more to do around here than you can imagine. It'll take a little more time. Just don't press me, okay?"

Overwhelmed by his own work, Steve usually backed off. The last thing Steve wanted was to upset Tim and have to do the books himself. He could also empathize with what Tim was going through, given the practice's growth over the past year.

Late at night in his office, Steve would sometimes recall his first years out of school. He missed the simple life he and his family had shared. Then, as quickly as the thoughts came, they would vanish. He had work to do and no time for daydreaming. "Having my own practice is a great thing," he would remind himself. "I simply have to apply myself, as I did in school, and get on with the job. I have to work as hard as I always have when something needed to get done."

Steve began to live most of his life inside his head. He began to distrust his people. They never seemed to work hard enough or to care about his practice as much as he did. If he wanted to go get something done, he usually had to do it himself.

Then one day, the office manager, Clarissa, quit in a huff, frustrated by the amount of work that her boss was demanding of her. Steve was left with a desk full of papers and a telephone that wouldn't stop ringing.

Clueless about the work Clarissa had done, Steve was overwhelmed by having to pick up the pieces of a job he didn't understand. His world turned upside down. He felt like a stranger in his own practice.

Why had he been such a fool? Why hadn't he taken the time to learn what Clarissa did in the office? Why had he waited until now?

Ever the trouper, Steve plowed into Clarissa's job with everything he could muster. What he found shocked him. Clarissa's workspace was a disaster area! Her desk drawers were a jumble of papers, coins, pens, pencils, rubber bands, envelopes, business cards, fee slips, eye drops, and candy.

"What was she thinking?" Steve raged.

When he got home that night, even later than usual, he got into a shouting match with Peggy. He settled it by storming out of the house to get a drink. Didn't anybody understand him? Didn't anybody care what he was going through?

He returned home only when he was sure Peggy was asleep. He slept on the couch and left early in the morning, before anyone was awake. He was in no mood for questions or arguments.

When Steve got to his office the next morning, he immediately headed for the break room—maybe a hot cup of coffee could get rid of his throbbing headache.

What lessons can we draw from Steve and Peggy's story? I've said it once and I'll say it again: *Every business is a family business.* Your business profoundly touches all members of your family, even if they never set foot inside your office. Every business either gives to the family or takes from the family, just as individual family members do.

If the business takes more than it gives, the family is always the first to pay the price.

In order for Steve to free himself from the prison he created, he would first have to admit his vulnerability. He would have to confess to himself and his family that he really didn't know enough about his own practice and how to grow it.

Steve tried to do it all himself. Had he succeeded, had the practice supported his family in the style he imagined, he would have burst with pride. Instead, Steve unwittingly isolated himself, thereby achieving the exact opposite of what he sought.

He destroyed his life—and his family's life along with it.

Repeat after me: *Every business is a family business.*

Are you like Steve? I believe that all dentists share a common soul with him. You must learn that a business is only a business. It is not your life. But it is also true that your business can have a profoundly negative impact on your life unless you learn how to do it differently than most dentists do it—and definitely differently than Steve did it.

Steve's dental practice could have served his and his family's life. But for that to happen, he would have had to learn how to master his practice in a way that was completely foreign to him.

Instead, Steve's practice consumed him. Because he lacked a true understanding of the essential strategic thinking that would have allowed him to create something unique, Steve and his family were doomed from day one.

This book contains the secrets that Steve should have known. If you follow in Steve's footsteps, prepare to have your life and business fall apart. But if you apply the principles we'll discuss here, you can avoid a similar fate.

Let's start with the subject of *money*. But, before we do, let's read the dentist's view about the story I just told you. Let's talk about how it's your story to write by Al and Chris. ❧

CHAPTER 2

It's Your Story – Gaining Some Perspective

Dr. Alan Kwong Hing
Christopher Barrow

Life is like a game of cards. The hand that is dealt you represents determinism; the way you play it is free will.

—Jawaharal Nehru

The basic premise that Michael Gerber puts forward is played out in dentistry on a daily basis. That is that you go to dental school for four or more years and learn to play with teeth and gums, but there is no point where anyone takes you aside and tells you there is a one-in-three chance that you will one day be running your own business! Even if you never own your own practice throughout the course of your career, business training is just as important, as in most cases you will work as a self-employed subcontractor—effectively your own one-man or one-woman business.

The strange thing about dental schools is that the professors seem to make out that it's almost criminal to earn money by doing dentistry. This attitude completely overlooks one of the main

9

reasons people become dentists in the first place. Of course you decided to become a dentist to help those in pain, but chances are you also wanted to be a dentist as it is a stable, financially rewarding profession. It's strange, then, that throughout dental school there is never any real focus on the financial side at all. Never is there mention of how much to bill, what to bill, or even how to bill. The dental schools leave it up to you to learn all of this once you graduate.

This is why so many dentists out there come unglued once they set up and run their own business. They see themselves (with some justification) as dentists first, and business owners a distant second. In E-Myth terms, the technician personality takes over and most dental practice owners spend all their time looking at teeth and not enough time considering their practice's fundamental needs.

Doing It, Doing It, Doing It

Running a successful dental practice is no easy task. Like almost every other dentist out there, chances are you will be learning by trial and error, or as we like to call it, "the school of hard knocks." When it comes to lessons in dentistry, one of the biggest you will learn is just how much running a practice really costs. Michael will talk about this in more detail in the next chapter, but by the time you discover that staff, suppliers, and the practice loan end up eating 95 percent of your business turnover, you'll realize that you can't eat what you don't collect. Without careful planning and strategy, things can soon start to spiral out of control.

As anyone who's ever been in this situation will know, when you're operating in this way, you're in a continual day-to-day crisis management mode. When you're stuck in this position, the idea that you can put your head up above the battlements, take a look into the future and say, "Where am I actually going with this?" seems almost impossible. It's not that you don't want to do it—it's more that you just don't have the time and you are simply too busy "doing it, doing it, doing it!"

Time is a major issue here. As a new dental business owner, it's likely you will be doing over seven hours of clinical dentistry a day, isolated within a very close-knit, "introverted" environment. Then in all the spare hours around this—either at the beginning or end of the day, or even during your lunch breaks—you will try to do everything else. To make matters worse, very often you will be doing this on your own either because you either don't trust anyone else to do the work, or you don't have the cash flow to think about hiring people to do these things for you.

Sound familiar? Do you feel overworked, overstressed and under-valued? The sad thing is, many dentists, knowing what they know now, probably wouldn't have chosen to set up their own practice.

What the E-Myth philosophy does is encourage us all to pause for a moment, take a step back and ask ourselves, "Why am I doing this? What is my end game? What's the vision that I've got for the future of my business?" Unless you do this, the only thing actually have is a job. You're just going to turn up and do the same thing over and over again until you drop dead.

Consider this: one day you will leave your dental practice for the very last time. It will be a one-way journey and you'll never be coming back again. The question you need to ask yourself is do you want to be carried out on a stretcher because you've dropped dead in the middle of your surgery, or do you want to walk out of there having had a celebration party, with a very healthy, happy, and prosperous retirement to look forward to? If you just keep "doing it, doing it, doing it" as Michael famously says, then the balance of possibilities entails that your exit will most likely be made on the stretcher. You will just slump over the chair one day and that will be that.

The Family Business

Another crucial factor in the E-Myth philosophy is family. Regardless of whether or not any member of your family works for you in your business, each of you reading this has, in one shape or form, created a family business.

Yes, you read it right—a family business.

One thing you need to recognize early on in your business career is that your family is, and will always be, intrinsically tied to your working life. This is because ultimately, the people you work for are those people you leave behind each morning when you head out to your practice.

Take the example of our friend John who runs a very profitable private practice in the heart of London. Each day he would come in early, make a cup of coffee, and sit down to write some emails. One day, however, he picked up his laptop only to find he couldn't open it—the screen was fixed tight to the keyboard! No matter how hard he tried to pry it open, the screen just wouldn't budge. It wasn't until later that John discovered the source of his laptop dilemma: his seven-year-old son. When John asked his son what on earth had made him superglue his laptop shut, the little boy replied, "Daddy, you won't play football in the garden with me any more because you're always playing with your laptop. I'd like you to play football!"

Clearly in this case, our friend John completely missed the point of why he was working in the first place. He missed one of the central pillars of the E-Myth philosophy.

As Michael says, you need to take a step back and ask yourself why you're doing the things you do. Why are you working in the first place? Though we are both reasonably successful business people ourselves, even we have both been known to adopt technician tunnel vision at times—especially early in our careers.

A number of years ago now, Al used to fly into Nova Scotia every month to do a couple of days of surgery. His work was extremely intensive, and he would work long hours. He'd go in first thing in the morning, do dentistry all day, and then crash in a nearby hotel in the evening before getting up the next day to do the same all over again. He'd go on like this for a few more days before flying back out to his home in Toronto. Then, two years after he bought the practice and two years after he started practicing in Nova Scotia, Al found himself with some spare time. So, he decided to go for a little walk. After about half an hour he stopped and stared, shocked by what he saw. He had never realized his practice was by the sea! This wake up call illustrates how everyone needs to take a moment and evaluate what they are doing and why.

Both of our real life examples show the state people get themselves into when they lack an element of vision for their business. Time and time again we hear the same story from dentists. They come up to us and say, "Before I started my own business I'd do a day of dentistry, then I'd go to the gym, have a workout, then a swim and a sauna. I'd then go home, cook dinner, watch some TV, maybe have a pint. Now that I've opened my own business, I don't go to the gym any more, haven't swum in years, and those thin pants I used to wear are stuck in the wardrobe somewhere as I now wear the fat pants. It's the fat pants that go with owning your own business!'

What happens is, whether you're a dentist, an attorney, a chiropractor or other professional, as soon as you open your own business you create a monster. It's actually very much like a small baby. It screams all night and keeps you awake. When it's hungry it sucks you dry and when it's finished sucking you dry, it makes a mess all over you! A business behaves just like that if you don't take a long-term view. But worse—that business without a vision is like a baby that just doesn't grow up. It continues screaming and screaming and sucking you dry. Unless and until you step back, and unless and until you rise above the noise and the chaos, you will not be able to see where you are. Nor will you be able to see where you are going.

Do any of our real-life examples ring any bells with you? Don't worry if they do—there is still hope! The following chapters will give you the power to take back both your practice, and your life. Now then, would seem the perfect time to see what Michael has to say on the subject of money. ♣

CHAPTER

3

On the Subject of Money

Michael E. Gerber

There are three faithful friends: an old wife, an old dog, and ready money.
—Benjamin Franklin

Had Steve and Peggy first considered the subject of *money* as we will here, their lives could have been radically different.

Money is on the tip of every dentist's tongue, on the edge (or at the very center) of every dentist's thoughts, intruding on every part of a dentist's life.

With money consuming so much energy, why do so few dentists handle it well? Why was Steve, like so many dentists, willing to entrust his financial affairs to a relative stranger? Why is money scarce for most dentists? Why is there less money than expected? And yet the demand for money is *always* greater than anticipated.

What is it about money that is so elusive, so complicated, so difficult to control? Why is it that every dentist I've ever met hates to deal with the subject of money? Why are they almost always too late in

15

facing money problems? And why are they constantly obsessed with the desire for more of it?

Money—you can't live with it and you can't live without it. But you'd better understand it and get your people to understand it. Because until you do, money problems will eat your practice for lunch.

You don't need an accountant or financial planner to do this. You simply need to prod your people to relate to money very personally. From the person at the front desk to the hygienists, they all should understand the financial impact of what they do every day in relationship to the profit and loss of the practice.

And so you must teach your people to think like owners, not like technicians or office managers or receptionists. You must teach them to operate like personal profit centers, with a sense of how their work fits in with the practice as a whole.

You must involve everyone in the practice with the topic of money—how it works, where it goes, how much is left, and how much everybody gets at the end of the day. You also must teach them about the four kinds of money created by the practice.

The Four Kinds of Money

In the context of owning, operating, developing, and exiting from a dental practice, money can be split into four distinct, but highly integrated categories:

* Income
* Profit
* Flow
* Equity

Failure to distinguish how the four kinds of money play out in your practice is a surefire recipe for disaster.

Important Note: Do not talk to your accountants or bookkeepers about what follows; it will only confuse them and you. The information comes from the real-life experiences of thousands of small business owners, dentists included, most of whom were hopelessly confused about money when I met them. Once they understood and accepted the following principles, they developed a clarity about money that could only be called enlightened.

The First Kind of Money: Income

Income is the money dentists are paid by their practice for doing their job *in* the practice. It's what they get paid for going to work every day.

Clearly, if dentists didn't do their job, others would have to, and *they* would be paid the money the practice currently pays the dentists. Income, then, has nothing to do with *ownership*. Income is solely the province of *employeeship*.

That's why to the dentist-as-*employee*, income is the most important form money can take. To the dentist-as-*owner*, however, it is the least important form money can take.

Most important; least important. Do you see the conflict? The conflict between the dentist-as-employee and the dentist-as-owner?

We'll deal with this conflict later. For now, just know that it is potentially the most paralyzing conflict in a dentist's life.

Failing to resolve this conflict will cripple you. Resolving it will set you free.

The Second Kind of Money: Profit

Profit is what's left over after a dental practice has done its job effectively and efficiently. If there is no profit, the practice is doing something wrong.

However, just because the practice shows a profit does not mean it is necessarily doing all the right things in the right way. Instead, it just means that something was done right during or preceding the period in which the profit was earned.

The important issue here is whether the profit was intentional or accidental. If it happened by accident (which most profit does), don't take credit for it. You'll live to regret your impertinence.

If it happened intentionally, take all the credit you want. You've earned it. Because profit created intentionally, rather than by accident, is replicable—again and again. And your practice's ability to repeat its performance is the most critical ability it can have.

As you'll soon see, the value of money is a function of your practice's ability to produce it in predictable amounts at an above-average return on investment.

Profit can be understood only in the context of your practice's purpose, as opposed to your purpose as a dentist. Profit, then, fuels the forward motion of the practice that produces it. This is accomplished in four ways:

- Profit is *investment capital* that feeds and supports growth.
- Profit is *bonus capital* that rewards people for exceptional work.
- Profit is *operating capital* that shores up money shortfalls.
- Profit is *return-on-investment capital* that rewards you, the dentist-owner, for taking risks.

Without profit, a dental practice cannot subsist, much less grow. Profit is the fuel of progress.

If a practice misuses or abuses profit, however, the penalty is much like having no profit at all. Imagine the plight of a dentist who has way too much return-on-investment capital and not enough investment capital, bonus capital, and operating capital. Can you see the imbalance this creates?

The Third Kind of Money: Flow

Flow is what money *does* in a dental practice, as opposed to what money *is*. Whether the practice is large or small, money tends to move erratically through it, much like a pinball. One minute it's there; the next minute it's not.

Flow can be even more critical to a practice's survival than profit, because a practice can produce a profit and still be short of money. Has this ever happened to you? It's called profit on paper rather than in fact.

No matter how large your practice, if the money isn't there when it's needed, you're threatened—regardless of how much profit you've made. You can borrow it, of course. But money acquired in dire circumstances is almost always the most expensive kind of money you can get.

Knowing where the money is and where it will be when you need it is a critically important task of both the dentist-as-employee and the dentist-as-owner.

Rules of Flow

You will learn no more important lesson than the huge impact flow can have on the health and survival of your dental practice, let alone your business or enterprise. The following two rules will help you understand why this subject is so critical.

1. **The First Rule of Flow states that your income statement is static, while the flow is dynamic.** Your income statement is a snapshot, while the flow is a moving picture. So, while your income statement is an excellent tool for analyzing your practice *after* the fact, it's a poor tool for managing it in the heat of the moment.

Your income statement tells you (1) how much money you're spending and where, and (2) how much money you're receiving and from where.

Flow gives you the same information as the income statement, plus it tells you *when* you're spending and receiving money. In other words, flow is an income statement moving through time. And that is the key to understanding flow. It is about management in real time. How much is coming in? How much is going out? You'd like to know this daily, or even by the hour if possible. Never by the week or month.

You must be able to forecast flow. You must have a flow plan that helps you gain a clear vision of the money that's out there next month and the month after that. You must also pinpoint what your needs will be in the future.

Ultimately, however, when it comes to flow, the action is always in the moment. It's about *now*. The minute you start to meander away from the present, you'll miss the boat.

Unfortunately, few dentists pay any attention to flow until it dries up completely and slow pay becomes no pay. They are oblivious to this kind of detail until, say, patients announce that they won't pay for this or that. That gets a dentist's attention because the expenses keep on coming.

When it comes to flow, most dentists are flying by the proverbial seat of their pants. No matter how many people you hire to take care of your money, until you change the way you think about it, you will always be out of luck. No one can do this for you.

Managing flow takes attention to detail. But when flow is managed, your life takes on an incredible sheen. You're swimming with the current, not against it. You're in charge!

2. **The Second Rule of Flow states that money seldom moves as you expect it to.** But you do have the power to change that, provided you understand the two primary sources of money as it comes in and goes out of your dental practice.

The truth is, the more control you have over the *source* of money, the more control you have over its flow. The sources of money are both inside and outside your practice.

Money comes from *outside* your practice in the form of receivables, reimbursements, investments, and loans.

Money comes from *inside* your practice in the form of payables, taxes, capital investments, and payroll. These are the costs associated with attracting patients, delivering your services, operations, and so forth.

Few dentists see the money going *out* of their practice as a source of money, but it is.

When considering how to spend money in your practice, you can save—and therefore make—money in three ways:

- Do it more effectively.
- Do it more efficiently.
- Stop doing it altogether.

By identifying the money sources inside and outside your practice, and then applying these methods, you will be immeasurably better at controlling the flow in your practice.

But what are these sources? They include how you

- manage your services;
- buy supplies and equipment;
- compensate your people;
- plan people's use of time;
- determine the direct cost of your services;
- increase the number of patients seen;
- manage your work;
- collect reimbursements and receivables; and
- countless more.

In fact, every task performed in your practice (and ones you haven't yet learned how to perform) can be done more efficiently and effectively, dramatically reducing the cost of doing business. In the process, you will create more income, produce more profit, and balance the flow.

The Fourth Kind of Money: Equity

Sadly, few dentists fully appreciate the value of equity in their dental practice. Yet equity is the second most valuable asset any dentist will ever possess. (The first most valuable asset is, of course, your life. More on that later.)

Equity is the financial value placed on your dental practice by a prospective buyer.

Thus, your *practice* is your most important product, not your services. Because your practice has the power to set you free. That's right. Once you sell your practice—providing you get what you want for it—you're free!

Of course, to enhance your equity, to increase your practice's value, you have to build it right. You have to build a practice that works.

A practice that can become a true business and a business that can become a true enterprise. A practice/business/enterprise that can produce income, profit, flow, and equity better than any other dentist's practice can.

To accomplish that, your practice must be designed so that it can do what it does systematically and predictably, every single time.

The Story of McDonald's

Let me tell you the most unlikely story anyone has ever told you about the successful building of a dental practice, business, and enterprise. Let me tell you the story of Ray Kroc.

You might be thinking, "What on earth does a hamburger stand have to do with my practice? I'm not in the hamburger business; I'm a dentist."

Yes, you are. But by practicing dentistry as you have been taught, you've abandoned any chance to expand your reach, help more patients, or improve your services the way they must be improved if the practice of dentistry—and your life—is going to be transformed.

In Ray Kroc's story lies the answer.

Kroc called his first McDonald's restaurant "a little money machine." That's why thousands of franchises bought it. And the reason it worked? Kroc demanded consistency, so that a hamburger in Philadelphia would be an advertisement for one in Peoria. In fact, no matter where you bought a McDonald's hamburger in the 1950s, the meat patty was guaranteed to weigh exactly 1.6 ounces, with a diameter of 3⅝ inches. It was in the McDonald's handbook.

Did Kroc succeed? You know he did! And so can you, once you understand his methods. Consider just one part of his story.

In 1954, Kroc made his living selling the five-spindle Multimixer milkshake machine. He heard about a hamburger stand in San Bernardino, California, that had eight of his machines in operation, meaning it could make forty shakes simultaneously. This he had to see.

Kroc flew from Chicago to Los Angeles, then drove 60 miles to San Bernardino. As he sat in his car outside Mac and Dick McDonald's restaurant, he watched as lunch customers lined up for bags of hamburgers.

In a revealing moment, Kroc approached a strawberry blonde in a yellow convertible. As he later described it, "It was not her sex appeal but the obvious relish with which she devoured the hamburger that made my pulse begin to hammer with excitement."

Passion.

In fact, it was the French fry that truly captured his heart. Before the 1950s, it was almost impossible to buy fries of consistent quality. Kroc changed all that. "The French fry," he once wrote, "would become almost sacrosanct for me, its preparation a ritual to be followed religiously."

Passion and preparation.

The potatoes had to be just so—top-quality Idaho russets, 8 ounces apiece, deep-fried to a golden brown, and salted with a shaker that, as Kroc put it, kept going "like a Salvation Army girl's tambourine."

As Kroc soon learned, potatoes too high in water content—even top-quality Idaho russets varied greatly in water content—will come out soggy when fried. And so Kroc sent out teams of workers, armed with hydrometers, to make sure all his suppliers were producing potatoes in the optimal solids range of 20 percent to 23 percent.

Preparation and passion. Passion and preparation. Look those words up in the dictionary and you'll see Kroc's picture. Can you envision your picture there?

Do you understand what Kroc did? Do you see why he was able to sell thousands of franchises? Kroc knew the true value of equity, and, unlike Steve from our story, Kroc went to work *on* his business rather than *in* his business. He knew the hamburger wasn't his product—McDonald's was!

So what does *your* dental practice need to do to become a little money machine? What is the passion that will drive you to build a practice that works—a turnkey system like Ray Kroc's?

Equity and the Turnkey System

What's a turnkey system? And why is it so valuable to you? To better understand it, let's look at another example of a turnkey system that worked to perfection: the recordings of Frank Sinatra.

Frank Sinatra's records were to him as McDonald's restaurants were to Ray Kroc. They were part of a turnkey system that allowed Sinatra to sing to millions of people without having to be there himself.

Sinatra's recordings were a dependable turnkey system that worked predictably, systematically, automatically, and effortlessly to produce the same results every single time—no matter where they were played, and no matter who was listening.

Regardless of where Frank Sinatra was, his records just kept on producing income, profit, flow, and equity, over and over … and still do! Sinatra needed only to produce the prototype recording, and the system did the rest.

Kroc's McDonald's is another prototypical turnkey solution, addressing everything McDonald's needs to do in a basic, systematic way so that anyone properly trained by McDonald's can successfully reproduce the same results.

And this is where you'll realize your equity opportunity: in the way your company does business, in the way your company systematically does what you intend it to do, and in the development of your turnkey system—a system that works even in the hands of ordinary people (and dentists less experienced than you) to produce extraordinary results.

Remember:

- If you want to build vast equity in your practice, then go to work *on* your practice, building it into a business that works every single time.
- Go to work *on* your practice to build a totally integrated turnkey system that delivers exactly what you promised every single time.
- Go to work *on* your practice to package it and make it stand out from the dental practices you see everywhere else.

Here is the most important idea you will ever hear about your practice and what it can potentially provide for you:

The value of your equity is directly proportional to how well your practice works. And how well your practice works is directly proportional to the effectiveness of the systems you have put into place upon which the operation of your practice depends.

Whether money takes the form of income, profit, flow, or equity, the amount of it—and how much of it stays with you—invariably boils down to this. Money, happiness, life—it all depends on how well your practice works. Not on your people, not on you, but on the system.

Your practice holds the secret to more money. Are you ready to learn how to find it?

Earlier in this chapter, I alerted you to the inevitable conflict between the dentist-as-employee and the dentist-as-owner. It's a battle between the part of you working *in* the practice and the part of you working *on* the practice. Between the part of you working for income and the part of you working for equity.

Here's how to resolve this conflict:

- Be honest with yourself about whether you're filling *employee* shoes or *owner* shoes.
- As your practice's key employee, determine the most effective way to do the job you're doing, a*nd then document that job.*
- Once you've documented the job, create a strategy for replacing yourself with someone else (another dentist) who will then use your documented system exactly as you do.

- Have your new employees manage the newly delegated system. Improve the system by quantifying its effectiveness over time.

- Repeat this process throughout your practice wherever you catch yourself acting as employee rather than owner.

- Learn to distinguish between ownership work and employee-ship work every step of the way.

Master these methods, understand the difference between the four kinds of money, develop an interest in how money works in your practice . . . and then watch it flow in with the speed and efficiency of a perfectly delivered adjustment.

Now let's take another step in our strategic thinking process. Let's look at the subject of *planning*. But first, let's see what Al and Chris have to say about money. ❧

4

The Money Game

Dr. Alan Kwong Hing
Christopher Barrow

Money should be mastered, not served.

—Syrus, Maxims

L ike it or loathe it, money is everything in the modern world. Being in possession of money means the freedom to do what you want, when you want, with who you want, and with no constraints. Ask yourself, why did you choose to become a dentist? Aside from all the reasons that are socially relevant, no doubt you chose to be a dentist as it almost guarantees that you will earn a good income, which translates into a good living. How you define "living" is up to you; however, you should consider that money in itself doesn't change everything. It's what you do with money that counts.

As Michael so eloquently puts it, one of the most important aspects to the E-Myth philosophy is recognizing the two elements to your inner self. That is, acknowledging the conflict between the dentist-as-employee and the dentist-as-owner, understanding the conflict, and then resolving it. These two personalities look at money very differently. If you don't put the right one in charge of making the important decisions about money then nothing will change in your life.

The dentist-as-employee, for example, focuses on short-term gains and financial safety—it is a low-logic, high-emotion mode of thinking that rarely takes into account the big picture. The dentist-as-owner, however, is far more calculating and can make decisions based on high-logic and low-emotion. Where one of these personalities sees money as a pay packet, the other sees collected money as leverage—as an opportunity for the business to grow.

The key to this book, and the whole E-Myth way of thinking, then, is to encourage you to shed your employee mentality and start thinking about your business in a constructive and logical way.

From our own experience time and time again, we find what gets most dentists with money is a lack of appreciation for overheads and the business side to dentistry. By adopting some of the key principles Michael has spoken about, you can become one of the privileged few—the dentists who don't get stuck doing it, doing it, doing it; those dentists who own a business, not a job.

The Money Game

Imagine your business as a bath. There are two taps at one end, and there are a number of plugholes at the other. The first tap is called "income generated from sales" and the second tap is called "capital injected."

When you start a business off, you've got to fill the bath to a certain level because there's enough water to keep the bath going. The first thing you do then is open the "capital injection" tap. You've got to keep this first tap running for a while before you open the doors.

Once your business is ready to go, you can now turn on the "income generated from sales" tap. This means you're now doing some dentistry and you're getting paid for it. The "capital invested" tap is now switched off and you have the "income from sales" tap that is (hopefully) running at least seven hours a day, five days a week.

So now we go down to the plugholes. Interestingly, there are three plugholes instead of one—this is a strange bath after all! The first is capital expenditure, the second plughole is the operating costs of the business, and the third plughole is the costs that only occur when you do any dentistry. Of these three plugholes, one you can open and close, one you only open when you do dentistry, and one is always, inexorably, draining away.

So here's the game: if the water runs out of the bath, you're bust. It's a bit like the film *Speed,* only this time instead of Dennis Hopper playing the mad bomber, it's a bank manager who's looking over your shoulder telling you that if the water in the bath runs out, he'll repossess your house. If you knew you owned a bath like that, and if you knew that if the water ran out you were going to lose your business and your livelihood you'd certainly pay more attention to the bath!

It's true to say that in the mid-to-late part of the twentieth century, you could essentially turn up and do your job and there would be enough water in the bath. You'd just about get by, because the government, an insurance company, or the grateful public would keep on paying. This has all changed now. If you don't keep your eye on the taps and the plugs, there is a real danger the water in the bath will run out.

The problem that many dentists get into is that they focus too heavily on the billing side of things and not enough on the collections side of the balance sheet. They are just too concerned with what's coming in and not nearly concerned enough about what's going out. Similarly, all too often we find many dentists get caught up in the dentist-as-employee mindset. They see money in their practice account and think it's theirs to spend as they see fit. Very often, emotion takes over and they invest their precious income on shiny new toys for the practice that barely get used and only service to get in the way.

If this is you, then here's some advice: stop it, stop it now. Think like a dentist-as-owner; act like a dentist-as-owner. Get the best price possible on goods and sundries. Rationalize big investments and budget for important costs such as staff training. Remember, you are a rational businessperson now—so start acting like one!

Budgeting, Budgeting, Budgeting

In order to maximize the profitability of your practice, budgeting is essential. In many instances, saving a dollar is far easier than trying to bill and collect more. This is why attention to the small expenses can help contain overheads. For example, if a dentist can save 1 percent per year on supplies and the office brings in $500,000 per year, that can amount to $5,000 of savings per year. Over a twenty-five-year career, this figure equates to $125,000. That is a lot of money for a small amount of saving. It can mean retiring a year earlier or taking an extra vacation every year upon retirement.

Of course, budgeting is tied in quite closely with planning—a subject Michael will expand upon in the next chapter—but we also need to remember one other important element to the budget: your family.

As we have already said, every business is a family business. Going back to our bath analogy for a moment, then, we haven't yet taken into account the fact that once a month, Mr. or Mrs. Dentist will come along with little dentist children and will take a bucket of water that they need!

As you can see, this whole money business is quite a complex game, and typically, it's a game dentists-as-business-owners are awful at playing. This is because most of the time, dentists are either too busy doing it, doing it, doing it, or they don't have systems in place to measure the flow of water in and out of the bath. You can be the most talented clinician in the world with the ability to do the most exquisite and complicated surgery, but at the end of the month, if you don't keep an eye on the bath, the bank can still turn up and repossess your house (Dennis Hopper—boom!).

The End Game

Of course, none of this is important unless you keep your eye on the prize. That is, you need to have your sights set firmly on the long-term, and what Michael describes as the end game.

In the previous chapter, Michael talks about the four types of money that make up the E-Myth philosophy. Of the four types of money, the most important is equity. That is, the value placed upon your practice by a prospective buyer. Equity is, therefore, the value of the product you create—the value of that which you hope to sell come retirement, or a return on all the years you've invested into your business.

And remember: it's a business. Your dental practice isn't about YOU, it's about the BUSINESS. If you create a product based solely around yourself, then come retirement you will have nothing to sell as, simply put, you won't be there to keep the product going!

This reminds us of a colleague of ours who used to work in a large city in Canada. Over the course of his career he developed an incredible skill set and had built a bespoke practice where patients had to be invited to join. He worked four days per week with two staff and had all the latest and greatest of bright, shiny objects to impress his patients and allow him to deliver great dentistry. He had considerable experience and had developed a strong niche market. In fact, he was earning more in a month than most people earn in a year! Due to a change in his family situation, however, he had to move out of the province, but was faced with a problem: He had a great practice but it was all about him. As a result, he could not sell the office after many years on the market and at a very fair price. He ended up closing shop with no buyer at all! All his years of planning and success to build his fantastic practice were wasted, as there was no thought given to the end game!

I bet our poor colleague wishes he had considered the E-Myth philosophy sooner! Thankfully, by reading this book, you're putting yourself in the best position possible to make the most of your business and the equity you hope to achieve in the end.

So, have you thought about your end game? If you haven't just yet, don't worry—there's still plenty of time to turn things around! On that note, now would seem the perfect time to see what Michael has to say about planning. ❧

On the Subject
of Planning

Michael E. Gerber

Luck is good planning, carefully executed.

—Anonymous

Another obvious oversight revealed in Steve and Peggy's story was the absence of true planning.

Every dentist starting his or her own practice must have a plan. You should never begin to see patients without a plan in place. But, like Steve, most dentists do exactly that.

A dentist lacking a vision is simply someone who goes to work every day. Someone who is just doing it, doing it, doing it. Busy, busy, busy. Maybe making money, maybe not. Maybe getting something out of life, maybe not. Taking chances without really taking control.

The plan tells anyone who needs to know *how we do things here*. The plan defines the objective and the process by which you will attain it. The plan encourages you to organize tasks into functions, and then helps people grasp the logic of each of those functions. This in turn permits you to bring new employees up to speed quickly.

There are numerous books and seminars on the subject of practice management, but they focus on making you a better dentist. I want to teach you something else that you've never been taught before: how to be a manager. It has nothing to do with conventional practice management and everything to do with thinking like an entrepreneur.

The Planning Triangle

As we discussed in the Preface, every dental practice is a company, every dental business is a company, and every dental enterprise is a company. Yet the difference between the three is extraordinary. Although all three may offer dental services, how they do what they do is completely different.

The trouble with most companies owned by dentists is that they are dependent on the dentist. That's because they're a practice—the smallest, most limited form a company can take. Practices are formed around the technician, whether dentist or roofer.

You may choose in the beginning to form a practice, but you should understand its limitations. The company called a *practice* depends on the owner—that is, the dentist. The company called a *business* depends on other people plus a system by which that business does what it does. Once your practice becomes a business, you can replicate it, turning it into an *enterprise*.

Consider the example of Sea Dentistry. The patients don't come in asking for Dr. Douglas Sea, although he is one of the top dentists around. After all, he can only handle so many cases a day and be in only one location at a time.

Yet he wants to offer his high-quality services to more people in the community. If he has reliable systems in place—systems that any qualified associate dentist can learn to use—he has created a business and it can be replicated. Douglas can then go on to offer his services—which demand his guidance, not his presence—in a multitude of different settings. He can open dozens of dental practices, none of which need Dr. Douglas Sea himself, except in the role of entrepreneur.

Is your dental company going to be a practice, a business, or an enterprise? Planning is crucial to answering this all-important question. Whatever you choose to do must be communicated by your plan, which is really three interrelated plans in one. We call it the Planning Triangle, and it looks like this:

- The Business Plan;
- The Practice; and
- The Completion Plan.

The three plans form a triangle, with the business plan at the base, the deal plan in the center, and the completion plan at the apex.

The business plan determines *who* you are (the business), the practice plan determines *what* you do (the specific focus of your dental practice), and the completion plan determines *how* you do it (the fulfillment process).

By looking at the Planning Triangle, we see that the three critical plans are interconnected. The connection between them is established by asking the following questions:

1. Who are we?
2. What do we do?
3. How do we do it?

Who are we? is purely a strategic question.

What do we do? is both a strategic and a tactical question.

How do we do it? is both a strategic and a tactical question.

Strategic questions shape the vision and destiny of your business, of which your practice is only one essential component. Tactical questions turn that vision into reality. Thus, strategic questions provide the foundation for tactical questions, just as the base provides the foundation for the middle and apex of your Planning Triangle.

First ask: What do we do, and how do we do it *strategically?*

And then: What do we do, and how do we do it *practically?*

Let's look at how the three plans will help you develop your practice.

The Business Plan

Your business plan will determine what you choose to do in your dental practice and the way you choose to do it. Without a business plan, your practice can do little more than survive. And even that will take more than a little luck.

Without a business plan, you're treading water in a deep pool with no shore in sight. You're working against the natural flow.

I'm not talking about the traditional business plan that is taught in business schools. No, this business plan reads like a story—the most important story you will ever tell.

Your business plan must clearly describe

- the business you are creating;
- the purpose it will serve;

- the vision it will pursue;
- the process through which you will turn that vision into a reality; and
- the way money will be used to realize your vision.

Build your business plan with *business* language, not *practice* language (the language of the dentist). Make sure the plan focuses on matters of interest to your lenders and shareholders rather than just your technicians. It should rely on demographics and psychographics to tell you who buys and why; it should also include projections for return on investment and return on equity. Use it to detail both the market and the strategy through which you intend to become a leader in that market, not as a dentist but as a business enterprise.

The business plan, though absolutely essential, is only one of three critical plans every dentist needs to create and implement. Now let's take a look at the practice plan.

The Practice Plan

The practice plan includes everything a dentist needs to know, have, and do in order to deliver his or her promise to a patient on time, every time.

Every task should prompt you to ask three questions:

1. What do I need to know?
2. What do I need to have?
3. What do I need to do?

What Do I Need to *Know?*

What information do I need to satisfy my promise on time, every time, exactly as promised? In order to recognize what you need to know, you must understand the expectations of others, including your patients, your associates, and other employees. Are you clear on those expectations? Don't make the mistake of assuming you know. Instead, create a need-to-know checklist to make sure you ask all the necessary questions.

A need-to-know checklist might look like this:

- What are the expectations of my patients?
- What are the expectations of my administrators?
- What are the expectations of my associate dentists?
- What are the expectations of my staff?

What Do I Need to *Have?*

This question raises the issue of resources—namely, money, people, and time. If you don't have enough money to finance operations, how can you fulfill those expectations without creating cash-flow problems? If you don't have enough trained people, what happens then? And if you don't have enough time to manage your practice, what happens when you can't be in two places at once?

Don't assume that you can get what you need when you need it. Most often, you can't. And even if you can get what you need at the last minute, you'll pay dearly for it.

What Do I Need to *Do?*

The focus here is on actions to be started and finished. What do I need to do to fulfill the expectations of this patient on time, every time, exactly as promised? For example, what exactly are the steps to perform when seeing someone with gum disease and related health conditions, or when designing the right care plan?

Your patients fall into distinct categories, and those categories make up your practice. The best dental practices will invariably focus on fewer and fewer categories as they discover the importance of doing one thing better than anyone else.

Answering the question *What do I need to do?* demands a series of action plans, including

- the objective to be achieved;
- the standards by which you will know that the objective has been achieved;
- the benchmarks you need to reach in order for the objective to be achieved;
- the function/person accountable for the completion of the benchmarks;
- the budget for the completion of each benchmark; and
- the time by which each benchmark must be completed.

Your action plans should become the foundation for the completion plan. And the reason you need completion plan is to ensure that everything you do is not only realistic but can also be managed.

The Completion Plan

If the practice plan gives you results and provides you with standards, the completion plan tells you everything you need to know about every benchmark in the practice plan—that is, how you're going to fulfill patient expectations on time, every time, as promised. In other words, how you're going to arrange a referral to another professional, conduct routine procedures, issue a recommendation, or educate a patient about dental erosion.

The completion plan is essentially the operations manual, providing information about the details of doing tactical work. It is a guide to tell the people responsible for doing that work exactly how to do it.

Every completion plan becomes a part of the knowledge base of your business. No completion plan goes to waste. Every completion plan becomes a kind of textbook that explains to new employees or new associates joining your team how your practice operates in a way that distinguishes it from all other dental practices.

To return to an earlier example, the completion plan for making a Big Mac is explicitly described in the *McDonald's Operation Manual*, as is every completion plan needed to run a McDonald's business.

The completion plan for a dentist might include the step-by-step details of how to analyze the physiological aspects of a patient's teeth using the best clinical practice evidence—in contrast to how everyone else has learned to do it. Of course, every doctor of dentistry has been taught a dozen methods to analyze a tooth. They've learned to do it the same way everyone else has learned to do it. But if you are going to stand out as unique in the minds of your patients, employees, and others, you must invent your own way of doing even ordinary things. Most of that value-added perception will come from your communication skills, your listening skills, your innovative skills in transforming an ordinary visit into a patient experience.

Perhaps you'll decide that a mandatory part of your root canal procedure is to print out the completed analysis and show it to the patient, explaining what the procedure is so that she has a better understanding of the operation. If no other dentist your patient has seen has ever taken the time to explain the procedure, you'll immediately set yourself apart. You must constantly raise the questions: *How do we do it here? How should we do it here?*

The quality of your answers will determine how effectively you distinguish your practice from every other dentist's practice.

Benchmarks

You can measure the movement of your practice—from what it is today to what it will be in the future—using business benchmarks. These are the goals you want your business to achieve during its lifetime.

Your benchmarks should include the following:

- Financial benchmarks
- Emotional benchmarks (the impact your practice will have on everyone who comes into contact with it)

- Performance benchmarks
- Patient benchmarks (Who are they? Why do they come to you? What does your practice give them that no one else does?)
- Employee benchmarks (How do you grow people? How do you find people who want to grow? How do you create a school in your practice that will teach your people skills they can't learn anywhere else?)

Your business benchmarks will reflect (1) the position your practice will hold in the minds and hearts of your patients, employees, and investors; and (2) how you intend to make that position a reality through the systems you develop.

Your benchmarks will describe how your management team will take shape and what systems you will need to develop so that your managers, just like McDonald's managers, will be able to produce the results for which they will be held accountable.

Benefits of the Planning Triangle

By implementing the Planning Triangle, you will discover:

- what your practice will look, act, and feel like when it's fully evolved;
- when that's going to happen;
- how much money you will make; and
- much, much more.

These, then, are the primary purposes of the three critical plans: (1) to clarify precisely what needs to be done to get what the dentist wants from his or her practice and life, and (2) to define the specific steps by which it will happen.

First *this* must happen, then *that* must happen. One, two, three. By monitoring your progress, step-by-step, you can determine whether you're on the right track.

That's what planning is all about. It's about creating a standard—a yardstick—against which you will be able to measure your performance.

Failing to create such a standard is like throwing a straw into a hurricane. Who knows where that straw will land?

Have you taken the leap? Have you accepted that the word *business* and the word *practice* are not synonymous? That a practice relies on the dentist and a business relies on other people plus a system?

Because most dentists are control freaks, 99 percent of today's dental companies are practices, not businesses.

The result, as a friend of mine says, is that "dentists are spending all day stamping out fires when all around them the forest is ablaze. They're out of touch, and that dentist better take control of the practice before someone else does."

Because dentists are never taught to think like businesspeople, the health-care professional is forever at war with the business-person. This is especially evident in large, multidiscipline practices, where bureaucrats (businesspeople) often try to control dentists (health-care professionals). They usually end up treating each other as combatants. In fact, the single greatest reason dentists become entrepreneurs is to divorce such bureaucrats and to begin to reinvent the dental enterprise.

That's you. Now the divorce is over and a new love affair has begun. You're a dentist with a plan! Who wouldn't want to do business with such a person?

Now let's take the next step in our strategic odyssey. Let's take a closer look at the subject of *management*. But before we do, let's see what Al and Chris have to say about planning. ❧

CHAPTER 6

Planning a Course to Success

Dr. Alan Kwong Hing
Christopher Barrow

The ability to convert ideas to things is the secret to outward success.
—Henry Ward Beecher

Whether you work in dentistry, accountancy, banking, or retail, planning is absolutely essential to the success of *any* business. There is a saying that people don't plan to fail—they fail to plan. In a nutshell, this is the problem. Most people do not have a set of goals and have not set themselves a life journey. More importantly, they have not decided to undertake a journey of success.

So why is planning so important? Imagine you are taking part in a yacht race across the Atlantic. In order to save weight, you decide to leave the navigator behind. While your crew may be sailing as hard as they possibly can, without a navigator taking positional readings on a regular basis you don't actually know where you're going! This means you can have two identical yachts with two identical crews, but one yacht will end up at the finish line, and the other one won't!

A dental practice is rather like a yacht—it's susceptible to external influences just like a yacht (such as the wind and the tide), and is also susceptible to internal conditions such as the trim of the boat and the set of the sail.

In business, if everybody just shows up and works as hard as they can each and every day, they can keep on working and working, but without someone taking regular readings, the crew will just work the business into insolvency. This is why it's so essential that when you have a business, you thoroughly plan your course before you set off (taking into account any factors that may knock you off course), and you take regular readings along the way to check that you're still heading in the right direction. If at any point you do find you're not on the correct course, it's essential that you adjust to get back on track!

Failing to Plan = Planning to Fail

One of the principle reasons businesses fail in dentistry is not because people are not working hard enough, but simply because the people in them are not plotting a course in the first place or are not taking a positional reading to see where they're up to. It beggars belief that this would happen, but experience tells us that at least 80 percent of practices out there are sailing under no specific direction and are opening themselves up to the ravages of luck.

As Michael so rightly says, planning is absolutely essential to any business. As the owner of your practice, it is your vision, planning, and management that will shape its destiny. Your decisions will ultimately decide whether your practice sinks or swims.

Scary thought isn't it? Thankfully, help is at hand. Armed with Michael's Planning Triangle you will be in the best position possible to set your business on course to success.

So where to start? Well, very early on, you will need to sit down and get your personal planning in place. For years as an undergraduate you will have set yourself regular goals—be it passing an exam or completing an assignment—so now you are a practice owner, you need to sit down with your significant other (if you have one) and decide upon a set of goals that you should reassess regularly. Once you have a system of *personal* planning in place, in many respects, the Planning Triangle is a natural progression.

The Secret to Good Planning

It's important to remember here that when it comes to good, proper business planning, there really is no need to reinvent the wheel. There's a whole world of information out there for you to draw upon that is readily available in any good book store or library. Once you have completed research and self-education, you can then sit down and start applying what you've learned, and what you've decided upon, to Michael's Planning Triangle.

At its heart the Planning Triangle asks three key questions:

- Who are you? (the business plan)
- What do you do? (the practice plan)
- How do you do it? (the completion plan)

Each of these questions should be an important pillar in building your practice. Each question helps you to develop your story—a detailed outline of your vision and how you're going to achieve it.

If you're reading this and haven't yet bought your own practice, you need to consider that your final business plan will depend very much on how you plan to set up your business. Are you, for example, buying an existing practice, or taking up a private squat? Each approach has its own advantages and pitfalls and requires thorough planning regarding either the old dentist's exit strategy, or how on earth you're going to fill your patient book from scratch!

One thing you should always remember when planning is that a good plan should always be flexible. Of course you will need targets and timelines to work towards as we all need a benchmark; however, many issues will arise that will require you to modify your plan. For example, if you attend a seminar on how to grow your new patient flow via a regular blog posting and new website, the anticipation might be that you achieve ten new patients a month as a result of this. If this figure turns out to be overly optimistic then it may be time for a new plan. If it works then keep doing what you are doing!

The Review Process

Naturally, it is also important to decide *when* you should assess if your planning has been successful or not. Depending on the nature of the plan, this can be a daily issue—such as planning for X amount of production per day. If you hit the target, then you must assess why you met the target and how you might be able to repeat it. If you don't meet the target, then you should consider why the target was missed and adjust accordingly.

It might also be beneficial to adopt a longer-term view plan that may be a goal to increase the number of new patients referred as a result of a business-networking group. To expect immediate results may be difficult, and it may take a number of months to see if there is a positive effect from your monthly breakfast network meetings.

So, deciding when to review your plans is a result of:

1. Your own level of comfort on the reporting of results
2. Your willingness to initiate changes
3. Your willingness on how quick you want to make changes
4. What the thing you are monitoring is all about
5. The financial commitment or spending required to make things happen

The People Factor

On the subject of good business planning, we really do need to pause a moment and consider that most vital of resources: people.

Though Michael will explore the issue in greater depth in later chapters, people are an absolutely essential part of any plan, and can be a valuable asset that helps your business to thrive. You will of course need to get the right people to work for you, and furthermore, you will need to find the right people to employ for services such as accountancy and finance.

Once you have assembled your team of advisors, again, as part of embracing change in your plans, you need to make sure that the services you are getting from them are good for you. If not, then make new plans to get new advisors. Nothing should be static in business, and you should remember that you are paying your advisors and they are working for *you*, so make sure it is always you who is driving the bus!

Mentors are also an extremely important part of plan development. Ask yourself, who has mentored you in your development as a dentist? Who has inspired you and given you advice along the way? By reflecting on ourselves, and the people we have met in our lives, we can learn a great deal that we can apply to our own business practices. This can include ways of dealing with people and even useful systems for dealing with situations that crop up during the working day. All of these things should be considered when forming the wider plan for your practice and the management of your business.

Remember, nothing works better than emulating success. Once you have defined what success means to you then go out and find the people who have done it, then engage them in discussion—they may even find it refreshing! You know it's remarkable that very few people ever think to ask for personal advice on how to achieve success. If anyone came up to Al at one of his lectures and asked him how he has achieved what he has, he'd tell them for free! So the lesson is this: see who is doing what you want to do, and then seek them out for advice and guidance. You may be surprised at what reaction you receive!

So there you have it, planning the E-Myth way. The most important point to remember is that while without planning, you are lost on the sea of uncertainty, at the same time you should never take your plan for granted. As we all know, internal and external factors that impact upon your business are changing all the time. This is why it is so important to take a step back and reassess your plans—to regularly monitor your business so you can steer it on the course to success.

As we have seen then, there is always hope when there is a plan. Are you feeling that sense of urgency? Now that your plan is coming together, it's the perfect time to see what Michael has to say about management. ✤

On the Subject of Management

Michael E. Gerber

"Management" means, in the last analysis, the substitution of thought for brawn and muscle, of knowledge for folklore and superstition, and of cooperation for force.

—Peter F. Drucker, *People and Performance*

Every dentist, including Steve, eventually faces the issues of management. Most face it badly.

Why are so few able to get their dental practice to work the way they want it to and to run it on time? Why are their managers (if they have any) seemingly so inept?

There are two main problems. First, the dentist usually abdicates accountability for management by hiring an office manager. Thus, the dentist is working hand in glove with someone who is supposed to do the managing. But the dentist is unmanageable himself!

The dentist doesn't think like a manager because he doesn't think he is a manager. He's a dentist! He rules the roost. And so he gets the office manager to take care of stuff like scheduling appointments, keeping his calendar, collecting receivables, hiring/firing, and much more.

Second, no matter who does the managing, they usually have a completely dysfunctional idea of what it means to manage. They're trying to manage people, contrary to what is needed.

We often hear that a good manager must be a "people person." Someone who loves to nourish, figure out, support, care for, teach, baby, monitor, mentor, direct, track, motivate, and, if all else fails, threaten or beat up her people.

Don't believe it. Management has far less to do with people than you've been led to believe.

In fact, despite the claims of every management book written by management gurus (who have seldom managed anything), no one—with the exception of a few bloodthirsty tyrants—has ever learned how to manage people.

And the reason is simple: *People are almost impossible to manage.*

Yes, it's true. People are unmanageable. They're inconsistent, unpredictable, unchangeable, unrepentant, irrepressible, and generally impossible.

Doesn't knowing this make you feel better? Now you understand why you've had all those problems! Do you feel the relief, the heavy stone lifted from your chest?

The time has come to fully understand what management is really all about. Rather than managing *people*, management is really all about managing a *process*, a step-by-step way of doing things, which, combined with other processes, becomes a system. For example:

- The process for on-time scheduling
- The process for answering the telephone
- The process for greeting a patient
- The process for organizing patient files

Thus, a process is the step-by-step way of doing something over time. Considered as a whole, these processes are a system:

- The on-time scheduling system
- The telephone answering system
- The patient greeting system
- The file organization system

Instead of managing people, then, the truly effective manager has been taught a system for managing a process through which people get things done.

More precisely, managers and their people, *together*, manage the processes—the systems—that comprise your business. Management is less about *who* gets things done in your business than about *how* things get done.

In fact, great managers are not fascinated with people, but with how things get done through people. Great managers are masters at figuring out how to get things done effectively and efficiently through people using extraordinary systems.

Great managers constantly ask key questions, such as:

- What is the result we intend to produce?
- Are we producing that result every single time?
- If we're not producing that result every single time, why not?
- If we are producing that result every single time, how could we produce even better results?
- Do we lack a system? If so, what would that system look like if we were to create it?
- If we have a system, why aren't we using it?

And so forth.

In short, a great manager can leave the office fully assured that it will run at least as well as it does when he or she is physically in the room.

Great managers are those who use a great management system. A system that shouts, "This is *how* we manage here." Not "This is *who* manages here."

In a truly effective company, how you manage is always more important than who manages. Provided a system is in place, how you manage is transferable, whereas who manages isn't. *How* you manage can be taught, whereas *who* manages can't be.

When a company is dependent on *who* manages—Katie, Kim, or Kevin—that business is in serious jeopardy. Because when Katie, Kim, or Kevin leaves, that business has to start over again. What an enormous waste of time and resources!

Even worse, when a company is dependent on *who* manages, you can bet all the managers in that business are doing their own thing. What could be more unproductive than ten managers who each manage in a unique way? How in the world could you possibly manage those managers?

The answer is: You can't. Because it takes you right back to trying to manage *people* again.

And, as I hope you now know, that's impossible.

In this chapter, I often refer to managers in the plural. I know that most dentists only have one manager—the office manager. And so you may be thinking that a management system isn't so important in a small dental practice. After all, the office manager does whatever an office manager does (and thank God, because you don't want to do it).

But if your practice is ever going to turn into the business it could become, and if that business is ever going to turn into the enterprise of your dreams, then the questions you ask about how the office manager manages your affairs are critical ones. Because until you come to grips with your dual role as owner and key employee, and the relationship your manager has to those two roles, your practice/business/enterprise will never realize its potential. Thus the need for a management system.

Management System

What, then, is a management system?

The E-Myth says that a management system is the method by which every manager innovates, quantifies, orchestrates, and then monitors the systems through which your practice produces the results you expect.

According to the E-Myth, a manager's job is simple:

A manager's job is to invent the systems through which the owner's vision is consistently and faithfully manifested at the operating level of the business.

Which brings us right back to the purpose of your business and the need for an entrepreneurial vision.

Are you beginning to see what I'm trying to share with you? That your business is one single thing? And that all the subjects we're discussing here—money, planning, management, and so on—are all about doing one thing well?

That one thing is the one thing your practice is intended to do: distinguish your dental business from all others.

It is the manager's role to make certain it all fits. And it's your role as entrepreneur to make sure your manager knows what the business is supposed to look, act, and feel like when it's finally done. As clearly as you know how, you must convey to your manager what you know to be true—your vision, your picture of the business when it's finally done. In this way, your vision is translated into your manager's marching orders every day he or she reports to work.

Unless that vision is embraced by your manager, you and your people will suffer from the tyranny of routine. And your business will suffer from it, too.

Now let's move on to *people*. Because, as we know, it's people who are causing all our problems. But before we do, let's see what Al and Chris have to say about management. ❧

Management – Creating the Ideal Business Culture

Dr. Alan Kwong Hing
Christopher Barrow

What gets measured gets managed.

—Peter F. Drucker

Take a trip into your local bookstore and you'll find an overwhelming number of texts all promising to reveal the secrets of management and set you on the road to success. If you happen to read more than one of these management guides, chances are you will start to recognize a distinct trend between all of them. That's because just about every management guide out there translates into a message about motivating your employees.

But what if they're wrong, what if there's a different way? What if your people weren't the issue—what if it was your systems instead?

Look at it this way: when you're setting up your business, assigning tasks that you don't know how to do, or don't want to do may seem the easiest thing to do at first, but where does it leave you? It leaves you in a mess, that's where it leaves you! For instance, what should happen should your trusted office manager one day fall ill and go on sick leave? Does anyone else in the practice know how to fulfil the office manager's role? In all probability, the answer to this question will be no. That's because the job role relies too heavily on the individual, and not enough on systems.

And that's why the E-Myth way of thinking is so revolutionary. Instead of trying to manage a group of distinctly unique individuals—all of whom have their own set of ideas, motivators, and emotions—you can now manage a set of systems. Systems that are designed specifically by you.

Before we go any further, let's take a step back and remind ourselves of the E-Myth approach to management:

A manager's job is to invent the systems through which the owner's vision is consistently and faithfully manifested at the operating level of the business.

What this quite remarkable piece of thinking tells us is that it's your job as manager to create the systems by which your vision can be realized. If you want your telephones answered a certain way it's no good trying to micromanage each member of staff to change their responses until you achieve your goal. No, it's your job to put in place a system by which every member of staff knows precisely how to answer the phone.

Management Systems and You

When you take the E-Myth approach and apply it to your working life, it's important that you remember that systems and culture are both closely allied. Systems create culture—culture reflects systems.

Think of it like this: the systems you have are "how" you do things; the culture you have is "why" you do things. Both the "how" and the "why" are then dictated by that most important of factors: *you.*

Any dental business across the world is always a significant reflection on the personality of the dentist in charge. That's why it's really important when you first start out to sit down and engage in a process of self-reflection, asking yourself who you are, what's important to you, and what you want your business to be.

The problem for many small practices is that when you work in an isolated one-man-band type situation it can be very difficult to take advantage of good management processes, be they cultural or systematic. This might be for any number of reasons, but is often because the dentist is stuck in a work-intensive rut and doesn't have enough time to focus working ON the business instead of IN the business. It's shocking to think that even now there are some practices turning over huge figures that aren't even computerized! Some are still even storing receipts in a box to send off to the accountant at the end of the year! If you've read any of our previous chapters, you will hopefully realize that this poor approach to planning and organization is a sure-fire way to under-achieve as a business. How on earth are these practices' managers supposed to gauge how well the practice is doing?!

In these cases, clearly there aren't the correct management *systems* in place, and similarly there are many practices out there without the best *culture* either.

Remember, as the leader of your dental practice, *how* you react to a certain situation sets a precedent and so sets the standard for how the practice operates. Take cash for example. In many societies there is a "culture of cash" where everyone wants a deal if they pay in cash (just look at what this did to Greece!). Imagine if a patient turned up to your practice and offered to pay you a large sum of cash, expecting you to issue no receipt and offer a discount for the work carried out. Would you do it?

Well, if you did then you'd have set the standard for what is acceptable in your practice. If, however, you take a stand and refuse such an offer, standing firm with your fees, then your staff will hopefully feel justifiably proud in the work the practice is providing and that you are not compromising who you are and what you do just for the money.

Systems vs. Culture

Imagine if you will, a set of axes. These axes intersect at the middle, creating a grid of four, equally sized sections or boxes. On the vertical axis you have a rating for systems marked out of ten, with one being the lowest score at the bottom of the axis and ten being for the businesses with the best systems at the top of the axis.

Similarly, across the horizontal axis, we have "culture." On the far left-hand side, we have businesses with "bad culture," and on the far right hand side we have businesses with the very "best culture."

Now, when you have the appropriate culture and systems in place, then you are up at that top right hand section of our grid / matrix as an "inspired business"—a business people aspire to work in. This is because you have excellent management systems and your culture is one that people love to work in and reflects excellently upon the company as a whole. This really is the ideal for what a business should be. Many people would consider companies such as Apple and Virgin to be in this section of the grid.

In the bottom right quadrant of our axes then, we have businesses where the culture is good and people enjoy working there, but in the absence of good systems, the company will probably run out of money. We're not going to name names for companies that exhibit poor traits that occupy this category, but I'm sure you could all probably name a few!

Similarly, if we now look at the left hand side of the grid, we have companies with poor company culture that either have very good systems, or very bad. Neither section of the grid on the left side reflects a company that is a particularly pleasant place to work, and if your company happens to fall in the bottom left section then there's every chance the business is going to fail.

Reflecting on our set of axes, it's imperative to remember that this balance of systems and culture is swayed by you and what you believe in. The best businesses will acknowledge the strengths and weaknesses that exist in culture and systems and will work to backfill these areas to close the gaps.

This can only be achieved when there is a culture of openness and acceptance of change. You have to be willing to accept that nothing is perfect, and there are always opportunities to learn and to grow. Because dentistry is a profession so governed by the personality and mindset of the dentist, each practice will of course find the perfect blend is different, but at the same time, in some things there is a very clear distinction between right and wrong.

Benchmarking Revisited

In his chapter on planning, Michael spoke about the importance of benchmarking. And now, here in the chapter on management, we find this central E-Myth philosophy crops up again.

For us, benchmarking is a fundamental part of our business operations. It helps us judge our success, and similarly it can help you build your business into something you've always wanted it to be.

In our mind, a great standard of exceptional business culture is the Four Seasons Hotel Group. Renowned as offering some of the most luxurious resorts anywhere in the world, Four Seasons' marketing material reflects a policy we think fits perfectly with dentistry. That is (and we quote): "In all our interactions with our guests, customers, business associates and colleagues, we seek to deal with others as we would have them deal with us."

Some of you may recognize the Four Seasons' approach as being closely aligned with the age-old notion of "do unto others as you would have others do unto you." But this isn't about religion—it's about fundamental human behaviour and gives a great insight into how many of the world's biggest, most successful businesses set about trying to build their corporate culture.

Virgin is another great example here. No one will ever get tired of reading stories about how Richard Branson gave up his seat for an old lady on one of his flights, or phoned an employee whose mother has been taken ill.

In this case in particular we see how systems and culture can work together with powerful effect. Of course Richard Branson doesn't know every one of his employees personally—that's impossible! But what Virgin does have is a great set of *systems* in place where by an assistant will have all the information to arrange for Mr. Branson to call. Though we must remember at its heart this is a system, it is also a system that both reflects and helps build a culture that values people, wherein employees feel valued and more motivated to do better for the business!

YOU are the Leader!

Looking back at our imaginary set of axes, the interesting thing about the healthcare sector is that the systems that are on that vertical axis are becoming more and more regulated, and dentistry in particular. In England, for example, there is the Care Quality Commission (CQC) that sets out guidelines in which dental practices must operate. It essentially assesses practices and the level of care they provide. In one respect then, the systematic side of dental management is increasingly becoming an issue of compliance.

But don't let this put you off! No amount of regulation will ever compensate for a business owner who themselves is the very example of the cultural standards of the business they have created around themselves. In all of this, remember, YOU are the leader. The way you dress, the way you behave, your attitude and the way you talk about other people sets the standard for everybody else in the workplace. YOU create the culture. If you want to change the culture, you must (as Ghandi once said) "become the change!" You must create the systems through which you can realize your practice vision.

On that note, now seems the perfect point at which to pause for a breath. We turn now to Michael, to see what he has to say on the subject of people. ✤

On the Subject
of People

Michael E. Gerber

*We are not human beings having a spiritual experience. We are spiritual
beings having a human experience.*

—Teilhard de Chardin

Every dentist I've ever met has complained about people.

About employees: "They come in late, they go home early,
they have the focus of an antique camera!"

About insurance companies: "They're living in a non-
parallel universe!"

About patients: "They want me to repair thirty years of bad
habits and inadequate oral hygiene!"

People, people, people. Every dentist's nemesis. And at the heart
of it all are the people who work for you.

"By the time I tell them how to do it, I could have done it twenty
times myself!" "How come nobody listens to what I say?" "Why is it
nobody ever does what I ask them to do?" Does this sound like you?

So what's the problem with people? To answer that, think back to the last time you walked into a dentist's office. What did you see in the people's faces?

Most people working in dentistry are harried. You can see it in their expressions. They're negative. They're bad-spirited. They're humorless. And with good reason. After all, they're surrounded by people who have toothaches, or are suffering from gingivitis, or—worst-case scenario—may even be a candidate for serious surgery. Patients are looking for nurturing, for empathy, for care. And many are either terrified or depressed. They don't want to be there.

Is it any wonder employees at most dental practices are disgruntled? They're surrounded by unhappy people all day. They're answering the same questions 24/7. And most of the time, the dentist has no time for them. He or she is too busy leading a dysfunctional life.

Working with people brings great joy—and monumental frustration. And so it is with dentists and their people. But why? And what can we do about it?

Let's look at the typical dentist—who this person is and isn't.

Most dentists are unprepared to use other people to get results. Not because they can't find people, but because they are fixated on getting the results themselves. In other words, most dentists are not the businesspeople they need to be, but *technicians suffering from an entrepreneurial seizure*.

Am I talking about you? What were you doing before you became an entrepreneur?

Were you an associate dentist working for a large multi-clinic organization? A midsized practice? A small practice?

Didn't you imagine owning your own practice as the way out?

Didn't you think that because you knew how to do the technical work—because you knew so much about orthodontics, general dentistry, and wellness—that you were automatically prepared to create a practice that does that type of work?

Didn't you figure that by creating your own practice, you could dump the boss once and for all? How else to get rid of that impossible person, the one driving you crazy, the one who never let you do your own thing, the one who was the main reason you decided to take the leap into a business of your own in the first place?

Didn't you start your own practice so that you could become your own boss?

And didn't you imagine that once you became your own boss, you would be free to do whatever you wanted to do—and to take home *all* the money?

Honestly, isn't that what you imagined? So you went into business for yourself and immediately dived into work.

Doing it, doing it, doing it.

Busy, busy, busy.

Until one day you realized (or maybe not) that you were doing all of the work. You were doing everything you knew how to do, plus a lot more you knew nothing about. Building sweat equity, you thought.

In reality, a technician suffering from an entrepreneurial seizure.

You were just hoping to make a buck in your own practice. And sometimes you did earn a wage. But other times you didn't. You were the one signing the checks, all right, but they went to other people.

Does this sound familiar? Is it driving you crazy?

Well, relax, because we're going to show you the right way to do it this time.

Read carefully. Be mindful of the moment. You are about to learn the secret you've been waiting for all your working life.

The People Law

It's critical to know this about the working life of dentists who own their own dental practice: *Without people, you don't own a practice, you own a job.* And it can be the worst job in the world because you're working for a lunatic! (Nothing personal—but we've got to face facts.)

Let me state what every dentist knows: Without people, you're going to have to do it all yourself. Without human help, you're doomed to try to do too much. This isn't a breakthrough idea, but it's amazing how many dentists ignore the truth. They end up knocking themselves out, ten to twelve hours a day. They try to do more, but less actually gets done.

The load can double you over and leave you panting. In addition to the work you're used to doing, you may also have to do the books. And the organizing. And the filing. You'll have to do the planning and the scheduling. When you own your own practice, the daily minutiae are never-ceasing—as I'm sure you've found out. Like painting the Golden Gate Bridge, it's endless. Which puts it beyond the realm of human possibility. Until you discover how to get it done by somebody else, it will continue on and on until you're a burned-out husk.

But with others helping you, things will start to drastically improve. If, that is, you truly understand how to engage people in the work you need them to do. When you learn how to do that, when you learn how to replace yourself with other people—people trained in your system—then your practice can really begin to grow. Only then will you begin to experience true freedom yourself.

What typically happens is that dentists, knowing they need help answering the phone, filing, and so on, go out and find people who can do these things. Once they delegate these duties, however, they rarely spend any time with the employee. Deep down they feel it's not important how these things get done; it's only important that they get done.

They fail to grasp the requirement for a system that makes people their greatest asset rather than their greatest liability. A system so reliable that if Chris dropped dead tomorrow, Leslie could do exactly what Chris did. That's where the People Law comes in.

The People Law says that each time you add a new person to your practice using an intelligent (turnkey) system that works, you expand your reach. And you can expand your reach almost infinitely! People allow you to be everywhere you want to be simultaneously, without actually having to be there in the flesh.

People are to a dentist what a record was to Frank Sinatra. A Sinatra record could be (and still is) played in a million places at the same time, regardless of where Frank was. And every record sale produced royalties for Sinatra (or his estate).

With the help of other people, Sinatra created a quality recording that faithfully replicated his unique talents, then made sure it was marketed and distributed, and the revenue managed.

Your people can do the same thing for you. All *you* need to do is to create a "recording"—a system—of your unique talents, your special way of practicing dentistry, and then replicate it, market it, distribute it, and manage the revenue.

Isn't that what successful businesspeople do? Make a "recording" of their most effective ways of doing business? In this way, they provide a turnkey solution to their patients' problems. A system solution that really works.

Doesn't your practice offer the same potential for you that records did for Sinatra (and now for his heirs)? The ability to produce income without having to go to work every day?

Isn't that what your people could be for you? The means by which your system for practicing dentistry could be faithfully replicated?

But first you've got to have a system. You have to create a unique way of doing business that you can teach to your people, that you can manage faithfully, and that you can replicate consistently, just like McDonald's.

Because without such a system, without such a "recording," without a unique way of doing business that really works, all you're left with is people doing their own thing. And that is almost always a recipe for chaos. Rather than guaranteeing consistency, it encourages mistake after mistake after mistake.

And isn't that how the problem started in the first place? People doing whatever they perceived they needed to do, regardless of what you wanted? People left to their own devices, with no regard for the costs of their behavior? The costs to you?

In other words, people without a system.

Can you imagine what would have happened to Frank Sinatra if he had followed that example? If every one of his recordings had been done differently? Imagine a million different versions of "My Way." It's unthinkable.

Would you buy a record like that? What if Frank were having a bad day? What if he had a sore throat?

Please hear this: The People Law is unforgiving. Without a systematic way of doing business, people are more often a liability than an asset. Unless you prepare, you'll find out too late which ones are which.

The People Law says that without a specific system for doing business; without a specific system for recruiting, hiring, and training your people to use that system; and without a specific system for managing and improving your systems, your practice will always be a crapshoot.

Do you want to roll the dice with your practice at stake? Unfortunately, that is what most dentists are doing.

The People Law also says that you can't effectively delegate your responsibilities unless you have something specific to delegate. And that something specific is a way of doing business that works!

Frank Sinatra is gone, but his voice lives on. And someone is still counting his royalties. That's because Sinatra had a system that worked.

Do you? Let's see if Al and Chris do, and then we will move on to the subject of associate dentists. ✤

CHAPTER 10

The People Problem

Dr. Alan Kwong Hing
Christopher Barrow

To rejoice in another's prosperity, is to give content to your own lot: to mitigate another's grief, is to alleviate or dispel your own.

—Thomas Edwards

When it comes down to team building, there is certainly no doubt that in our experience, trying to create a team of people who can work together in a dental practice is one of the biggest challenges that any principal faces. There are a number of reasons for this. One reason is that dentistry, like any healthcare profession, is a relatively high-pressure environment. This point ties in very closely with the second reason, that being that most dental practices receive a significant throughput of patients (or "customers") each day.

Ok, so if you're one of the lucky ones you may only see a couple of patients in the morning and a couple of patients in the afternoon, but this is far from the norm! Indeed, typically you can expect to see anywhere in the region of twenty-to-one-hundred patients per day, and sometimes in just one half-day session! So what you have then is a team of back-office staff, receptionists, telephonists, nurses and other members of the team all responding to the many varied needs of the hundreds of different patients who come through the door on a daily basis. If your team isn't up to the task, then this can make for a very tense, and often stressful, atmosphere that is in no way conducive to an effective business operation!

You should also consider the make-up of your team. Most people who will be working in the practice with you will be female. Though of course everyone should be treated equally, you do need to note that there is a difference in how men and women communicate. This then impacts upon the way team members interact with their supervisors. Women tend to respond differently to other women in managerial positions than they do if their supervisor is male.

To achieve more as a business you will need to hire someone who can manage a small or large group of females and do so with minimal stress with the rest of the team. If you don't have someone who can be trusted to manage and supervise team members, then, as Michael says, you will find yourself working as a technician suffering form an "entrepreneurial seizure" as you will be responsible for doing everything in the office!

Another problem with staffing that we should mention here is that historically, wages for team members have not always been brilliant. On the whole, dentists have never had a reputation for paying above average wages, as many dentists tend to see staff costs as a way of saving money in the business. The problem, however, is that lower wages tend to attract lower-capability people.

Put yourself in the position of your reception staff for a moment. If you were a well-qualified, highly motivated receptionist with great communication skills and a warm and friendly manner, you understand that your role is crucial to the success of the business. As such your skills have a value, and if you're a very good receptionist, then your value will be higher than that of other receptionists. Basic economics suggest that unless there are some major factors tying you down to a role, if you're offered more money down the road, chances are, you'll take it.

Another interesting point of note here is the importance of your reception staff as the "smiling face" of your business. Remember, your receptionist is the first person a patient sees when they come in to your practice. As such, it's important that they have an empathetic, mothering instinct, as (face the facts) most people who come into a dental practice are *scared*. Even if they haven't had a bad experience at the dentist's themselves, they probably know someone who has. This is evident even in the youngest children who often show up and the first thing they ask is, "Am I going to get a needle?" The ability to diffuse this anxiety takes a very special skill set. Once you have identified and hired these people, it is important to reward them both financially and with praise. As Michael says, without the right people you have to do it all yourself and you may not always be the right person to do the right thing. Therefore, when you have the right person for the job, make sure you retain them!

So, now you've had a chance to consider the arguments, ask yourself what's more important: saving money, or building the best team you can to provide the highest quality of care to your patients? We know which option we'd rather choose.

The Billable Time Conundrum

Compared to most other professions, dentistry is in a very special position. Even though you may be the practice owner, chances are you will spend most of your time locked inside your surgery, rarely if ever emerging into the outside world. So unless you specifically allocate time to come out of the surgery and communicate with your team members, then unfortunately that level of communication will not take place.

The problem here is that everyone in healthcare is obsessed with billable time. As a business owner, it's only natural that you should make the link between the patients you see and the money that you make. The difficulty is getting out of this mode of thinking to realize that it's only when you stop doing billable time that you can get together as a team and listen to how things are going.

This is why the business principles Michael teaches us are so important. By its very nature, dentistry encourages the technician mentality, but while you are busy doing it, doing it, doing it, you never get a chance to take a step back and work on your business; you never get a chance to take a step back and work on your team.

We've both spoken to many practice owners over the years who have said to us that they can't reduce the amount of billable hours they deliver and can't get people to stay behind after work, so as a result they don't have meetings. What people in this situation find, then, is that even if they do follow Michael's guidance on putting in place effective systems, over time these systems will deteriorate without sufficient care and attention.

There's an old cliché that a workforce is a group of people being forced to work together, and a team is a group of people working together to a common objective. In dentistry, it's fair to say there are far more "workforces" than "teams." Only by investing the time and the energy into your team can you really hope to make the very best success of your practice.

Recruiting the Right People

To quote Michael: "The People Law is unforgiving. Without a systematic way of doing business, people are more often a liability than an asset. Unless you prepare, you'll find out too late which ones are which." To build the perfect team, first you need to recruit the right people. Very early on in your recruitment system, you need to decide very clearly whether you want to take a quantitative approach to recruitment, or a qualitative approach.

A quantitative approach is where you seek out the cheapest people to work for you; a qualitative approach is where you seek out the best people.

The challenge is that most business owners will be tempted to take a quantitative approach as they want to keep costs down and so employ the least number of people in order to get the job done and to pay the lowest possible wages in order to get the job done. This is an example of scarcity mentality that is prevalent throughout dentistry and should be avoided if you want to build a business that you can be proud of. Whatever role you are hiring for, be it receptionist, telephonist, office clerk, or nurse, finding the right people for the right jobs will ultimately determine your success.

One of the most important lessons we can learn from Michael's excellent E-Myth philosophy is about systems. In his book *E-Myth Revisited*, Michael talks about building a recruitment system encompassing where to advertise for a job, how to advertise a job, what to say, and so on. The important point to remember here is that it isn't always necessary to use agencies to hire people. Your existing patients can be a very useful source of referrals, and will often provide you with better contacts than any agency or job board. This is because your patients are very often the ones who understand your business vision the best. After all, they're the ones who are on the 'receiving end'!

It's also useful to remember at this point that successful recruitment it not just about sticking an advert in the nearest dental journal and quoting an hourly rate of pay. Recruitment should be a far more focussed and targeted process. Spell out the exact specifications of the job and the characteristics of the type of person who is going to be most successful at this type of job, and most of all, don't settle for second best. The team of people you employ to work in your practice ultimately make your business. If you hire the wrong people, then your practice will only suffer as a result.

Too often dentists will hire a team member because they are "nice, young and pretty" and never systematically examine the unique skill set that is required for the role. For example, someone who does all the ordering of supplies has to be very organized and systematic, with a good attention to detail. Thus, each and every role in the practice requires a different personality to fit the bill correctly, and you must recognize these qualities in the hiring process. Most importantly though, once you have hired someone, you need to check on them and provide regular feedback on their progress and what they are doing.

Do you keep a regular check on your employees' performance? It's surprising just how few dentists do. For the best performance, again Michael's E-Myth philosophy comes up trumps, as the answer lies in systems. We recommend putting a system in place whereby you schedule regular formal evaluations of staff members either with yourself or a senior manager within the practice. After all, without regular reviews, how on earth are you supposed to know how well your staff are doing?

Training Your Staff: the Practice Handbook

In dentistry, training is absolutely essential. We now live in an age where professionals generally have to qualify for CPD credits. Though obviously this depends on where you live and what government regulations apply to your practice, you should never neglect your staff, be they clinical, or non-clinical. After all, the world is changing very rapidly, and dentistry is a fast-moving profession. Even a 2005 skill-set for a member of your admin or reception team can soon become out of date.

Aside from general training in terms of giving your team members the skills they need to actually do their jobs, Michael makes some excellent points when he talks about creating systems that take advantage of The People Law. Just like the Hilton Hotel chain, you should endeavour to create your very own brand standards manual by which members of staff can hope to realize your practice vision. This handbook should be updated regularly, and in it, you should establish what to do (a performance requirement), and the attitude with which it is done (a behavioural requirement). A combination of these performance and behavioural protocols will help you fully achieve this vision.

Naturally, the task of writing a handbook can seem quite daunting. That's why you should take a leaf from other businesses, and see what they've come up with. Reviewing several standard employee handbooks will give you a good grounding for where to start, and then it's just a matter of adding in your own extra details.

An important aspect for our own handbook is the treatment of staff and their families. What is the definition of a family? What work will be done at the practice? What about payment of lab fees? Though it may seem a trivial matter now, the treatment of staff and/or family members can become a big issue if guidelines aren't spelt out clearly very early on.

It's All Down To You!

Though your recruitment systems and practice handbook are of course both vital components in your people strategy, none of this will work without your leadership to guide the way. Not only is it your role as business owner to develop your strategy, it is also your duty to act as an example of your strategy in action.

As an example, we remember meeting one dentist in Birmingham who said to us that he'd been consistently six minutes late every day for fifteen years. Can you believe it?! The first thing to say about this dentist is that technically, he's not late—he's precisely on time! However, joking aside, in this example our colleague has created a protocol where everyone has to be at work for 9 a.m., but he will turn up at 9:06 a.m. From a performance perspective this is a ridiculous strategy as it automatically means the first patient is running late, and everyone else will run late in turn. Another point of note here is that the dentist's strategy is very divisive. After all, why should everyone else turn up at 9 a.m. if the dentist—the leader—is going to turn up at 9:06 a.m.?

The point here, then, is that leadership is important. As leader of your practice you should always meet the same performance requirements you set your staff. You create the standards and therefore you should behave in such a fashion that encourages people to meet the standards you set. Also remember, nothing should ever be below you. When Al set up his first practice, at the end of the day he would clean the toilets and take out the garbage. Even today, many years later, if things are running behind he will pitch in to clean up a room. The point here is that if you're going to inspire your team, then you have to lead by example! If things are running behind, then be prepared to muck in!

Are you ready for the challenge? Continue on to see what Michael has to say on the subject of associates. ♣

On the Subject of Associates

Michael E. Gerber

*Associate yourself with men of good quality if you esteem your own
reputation, for 'tis better to be alone than in bad company.*

—George Washington

If you're a sole practitioner—that is, you're selling only
yourself—then your dental company called a practice
will never make the leap to a dental company called a business. The progression from practice to business to enterprise
demands that you hire other dentists to do what you do (or
don't do).

Contractors call these people subcontractors; for our
purposes, we'll refer to them as associate dentists.

Contractors know that subs can be a huge problem. It's
no less true for dentists. Until you face this special business
problem, your practice will never become a business, and your
business will certainly never become an enterprise.

Long ago, God said, "Let there be dentists. And so they never forget who they are in my creation, let them be damned forever to hire people exactly like themselves." Enter the associates.

Merriam-Webster's Collegiate Dictionary, Eleventh Edition, defines *sub* as "under, below, secretly; inferior to." If associate dentists are like sub-dentists, you could define an associate as "an inferior individual contracted to perform part or all of another's contract."

In other words, you, the dentist, make a conscious decision to hire someone "inferior" to you to fulfill *your* commitment to *your* patient, for which you are ultimately and solely liable.

Why in the world do we do these things to ourselves? Where will this madness lead? It seems the blind are leading the blind, and the blind are paying others to do it. And when a dentist is blind, you *know* there's a problem!

It's time to step out of the darkness and come into the light. Forget about being Mr. Nice Guy—it's time to do things that work.

Solving the Associate Dentist Problem

Let's say you're about to hire an associate dentist. Someone who has specific skills: technique, rehab, whatever. It all starts with choosing the right personnel. After all, these are people to whom you are delegating your responsibility and for whose behavior you are completely liable. Do you really want to leave that choice to chance? Are you that much of a gambler? I doubt it.

If you've never worked with your new associate, how do you really know he or she is skilled? For that matter, what does "skilled" mean?

For you to make an intelligent decision about this associate dentist, you must have a working definition of the word *skilled*. Your challenge is to know *exactly* what your expectations are, then to make sure your other dentists operate with precisely the same expectations. Failure here almost assures a breakdown in your relationship.

I want you to write the following on a piece of paper: "By *skilled*, I mean . . . " Once you create your personal definition, it will become a standard for you and your practice, for your patients, and for your associate dentists.

A standard, according to *Webster's Eleventh,* is something "set up and established by authority as a rule for the measure of quantity, weight, extent, value, or quality."

Thus, your goal is to establish a measure of quality control, a standard of skill, which you will apply to all your associate dentists. More important, you are also setting a standard for the performance of your company.

By creating standards for your selection of other dentists—standards of skill, performance, integrity, financial stability, and experience—you have begun the powerful process of building a practice that can operate exactly as you expect it to.

By carefully thinking about exactly what to expect, you have already begun to improve your practice.

In this enlightened state, you will see the selection of your associates as an opportunity to define what you (1) intend to provide

for your patients, (2) expect from your employees, and (3) demand for your life.

Powerful stuff, isn't it? Are you up to it? Are you ready to feel your rising power?

Don't rest on your laurels just yet. Defining those standards is only the first step you need to take. The second step is to create an *associate dentist development system.*

An associate dentist development system is an action plan designed to tell you what you are looking for in an associate. It includes the exact benchmarks, accountabilities, timing of fulfillment, and budget you will assign to the process of looking for associate dentists, identifying them, recruiting them, interviewing them, training them, managing their work, auditing their performance, compensating them, reviewing them regularly, and terminating or rewarding them for their performance.

All of these things must be documented—actually *written down*—if they're going to make any difference to you, your associate dentists, your managers, or your bank account!

And then you've got to persist with that system, come hell or high water. Just as Ray Kroc did. Just as Walt Disney did. Just as Sam Walton did.

This leads us to our next topic of discussion: the subject of *estimating*. But first, let's press on to see what Al and Chris have to say on the subject of associate dentists. ♣

CHAPTER 12

Associates and You

Dr. Alan Kwong Hing
Christopher Barrow

If we do not plant knowledge when young, it will give us no shade when we are old.

—Lord Chesterfield

Michael is absolutely right when he talks about associates. Unless you want to remain a single-handed technician for the rest of your working life, then associates are destined to play an important part of your future.

Associates are something of a double-edged sword in dentistry, as so much of dentistry is based on relationships. Getting the wrong person in can be poisonous to the entire office, and will not only affect your patients, but your entire team. We have a friend who once had a substandard associate join his practice. Not only did our friend lose patients as a result, but when the associate quit he was left with problems that took over a year to correct!

79

All the goodwill our friend had spent years building up in a small community was lost in one bad decision. To make matters worse, as a consequence of his bad experience, when work started to get busier again, our friend was more content to run himself ragged than bring in another associate to help him out. The result was he suffered health-wise, and his levels of care were compromised with those he cared about the most: his patients.

But before we explore a little more about the art of dealing with associates, and how not to make the same mistake our friend did, first let's just take a step back and consider the context within which we are working here. Unlike many other professions, dentistry is in a fairly unique position as generally, globally, an associate dentist is a self-employed subcontractor. This is a very important point as it means as principal, technically you do not *employ* the associates working in your practice. This puts you in an interesting position and as a consequence, means that the relationship you have with your associates, and the relationship your other team members have with your associates is different to that of a normal employee. This is because your associates are effectively "independents" who are selling their time to you in exchange for a percentage of the fees generated. Thus the dynamic between associates and the practice as a whole is a little different to that outlined in many of Michael's other books.

But don't worry! Though the *dynamic* may be different, thankfully, all of Michael's fundamental principles still apply. With a little extra care and attention, soon your associates will see the E-Myth light, and your practice will be well and truly on the path to success!

Associates and the Art of Lead Generation

As a result of their unique employment status, it's very rare for a regular associate to get actively involved in lead generation. Though this may be something of a generalization, it's fair to say most associates expect to turn up in the morning and they expect patients to be waiting in the chair. Indeed, one of the main reasons people stay as associates is that they don't want to get involved in lead generation—that, and they don't want anything to do with the likes of compliance, government bureaucracy, and so on.

Another major hurdle you will find as principal is that many associates aren't especially interested in lead conversion either. What you will find, by and large, is that associate dentists will tend to deliver the work that is handed to them on a plate.

The problem here again links to dentistry's unique position compared to other healthcare services. If someone has a bad back, then they go to a chiropractic practice to find a solution to a bad back. Similarly, if someone has a sick cat, they go to the vets to make their cat better. In dentistry it's a very different business model. People can walk in with toothache—in which case it's just the same as with the vet or the chiropractor. However there is a whole product mix in dentistry that starts with relieving the toothache and then moves on to encompass long-term care, and can ultimately lead to high-end procedures such as cosmetics and implants. So, in terms of treatment planning you can literally have anything from $100 to an excess of $70,000!

A strange thing then occurs with your associate. As they get busier and bill more, they make more money. But as they don't understand the reality of practice ownership and the costs involved, they start to resent giving you back 60 percent of their fees. If they are particularly lucky they may have a 50 percent deal which is even better for them, however the reality is most dental practices run a 65-to-70 percent overhead, especially in large cities where the practice is actually losing money whenever the associate is working!

It has also been our experience that associates (even more so than practice owners) are reluctant to have any discussions with patients regarding money. In our travels and lectures around the world this seems to be one of the big dental hang-ups that the profession just can't seem to shake off. It's difficult to figure out why this may occur, but it does seem to come from the way dentists are educated to think of themselves as professionals, and as such should never discuss money with patients.

As dedicated followers of the E-Myth, we can all see the problem here, however the solution isn't always going to happen straight away. While the ultimate prize is still to generate and realize your equity come retirement, to create equity you need to manage your associates, and your business, in a very astute way. What you need to do then is hold fast to your E-Myth principles, and recognize that to effectively deal with your associates, you're going to need a combination of careful planning, gentle management, and a view to the long term.

Associates and You

When it comes to dealing with associates, the first piece of advice we can offer you is that associates are *not you*. If they were you then they would also be doing the hiring, so don't assume they will think the same way as you do.

A potential associate can be categorized in one of the following ways:

1. **Transitioning associate.** In this case the associate uses the time and experience working in your practice to learn the ropes prior to embarking on their own project. Very rarely do we see an associate who has been hired with the promise of an equity stake actually become a partner, so even if this carrot is dangled, it is rarely acted upon.

2. **Young career associate.** An associate who for various reasons does not want ownership due to debt levels, life freedom, and family choice. Typically, this associate is female, as in dentistry there are now more female dental students than male in many countries.

3. **Experienced career associate.** This is an associate who may have sold his/her practice and still has good health. They may have tried the retirement thing, but then came to realize that either they can't spend 24/7 with their

spouse, or you can only spend so much time sitting on the beach or playing golf. As a result they want to show up and do the dentistry that they still love, but have none of the headache of ownership.

4. **Malicious associate.** This is an associate who enters your practice or has been a previous associate or owner of the practice you purchased. They have one goal and that is to steal your patient base. As an associate they have been the only point of contact for the patient so they feel they have no loyalty to you as they have brought the patient into the office. It was, or becomes their goal, to move out—or across the road—and take their patients with them. This type of associate is one to watch out for. Make sure you trust your staff and also never lose touch with what is happening in the practice!

Before you can decide how best to deal with your associates, first you need to recognize their value, what they bring to your business, and how they work as part of your business model. Given some of the hurdles we have already outlined in this chapter, it is absolutely essential that you take these hurdles into account and factor them in to your business strategy.

The best way to do this is through effective planning. It is essential that you develop plans with your associate and treat them as a valued asset who you want to nurture and grow. Hopefully you have chosen well and they can become one of the exceptional associates who makes the transition into ownership.

We have already discussed planning and management in some detail in previous chapters, so if you feel perhaps you are still a little rusty on these areas, we do advise you go back and have another read through.

Now that you've well and truly established E-Myth principles in your mind, how are you going to address the associates conundrum?

One popular option many colleagues take is to upscale their business to build a large long-term care portfolio that can be managed by multiple associates. Another approach is to take a very different view and create a barrister's chamber effect with different specialists in each room. Alternatively, you can consider focusing your practice on a single specialist area, only employing specialist associates to provide a very niche service to the local community.

While there may yet be other options, these are three of the most common options we are starting to see emerge in dentistry. The first, and most popular option of these takes the "volume of patients = equity" approach, which can work for some practices, though this clearly isn't for everybody. Whichever option you go for in the end you need to remember that your associates are not technically your direct employees, so they need to be managed far more carefully than other employees.

Hiring and Acquiring

As if there wasn't already enough to think about in the world of associates, the next thing you need to consider is the dreaded H-word: hiring. Though the word may fill most employers (or potential employers) with dread, in dentistry, when it comes to hiring associates, again, we are in a very unique position.

Before you do anything, first you should consider the reasons you want an associate. Generally, the reasons for taking on a new associate fall into one of several different categories:

1. **You are too busy to service all your patients.** However, remember that it was you who made your practice grow in the first place. As such, your patients like and want to see you, so how you introduce the new associate to the existing patient base is important.

2. **You want to focus your skills in another direction.** It is important that in this relationship, your associate doesn't feel like they are only seeing the bad cases, or the patients who you don't want to see.

3. **You need a companion to discuss clinical things with during the day.** Although this sounds very nice, often you

are too busy to have chats, so maybe it is better for you to attend a study group that has no ties.

4. **You need to have someone in the office to work when you take time off, or don't want to work in the evening or at weekends.** If you manage your calendar and finances well, then this is not an issue, and as discussed before, most associates do not earn the practice money.

5. **You want to bring someone in to transition into ownership.** Although this may sound like a good option, generally it does not work out, as the parameters about when the associate acquires the rights to purchase, as well as a lack of clear goals, makes this process more damaging to the practice. Mainly this reason falls down the most due to lack of communication and monitoring of the associate's progress.

As with the hiring of non-dentist team members discussed in the previous few chapters, you really do need to have a system in place to deal with the hiring of associate team members. This system should account for both the associate's clinical skills, and their communication skills. We recommend an interview process whereby you can test to see how they drill, how they diagnose, and how they treatment plan. Have them present to your team a treatment plan after they do an initial interview with a patient. The longer the due diligence before hiring, then the greater the chances of your hiring the right person for the job.

Of course, while hiring may be an option, chances are you're more likely to *acquire* associates than hire them. Normally, if you should choose to start up your own practice, you have two options open to you: either you set up your own private practice from scratch, or you buy from a retiring principal. Unfortunately, starting from scratch can take years to achieve even a modicum of success, and can often cost more than most dentists can afford. As a result, we are seeing fewer and fewer new start-ups as it's far easier to buy in to an existing practice than start from scratch. As a result, very often dentists will more often than not acquire or inherit their associates as part of the practice package.

This is a very difficult process to manage as the associates in the new practice will feel that they have been at it for a while and they do not need any help. They resent being told what to do as they are, after all, independent practitioners. Although we have said the associate is not an employee, the level of expectation you should have with them is much higher than with a regular employee as they earn a lot more. They are also far more crucial than a regular team member to making you successful. As the new owner then you will need their support as well as their production to help you pay the large bill you have acquired from purchasing the practice in the first place. You cannot be too beholden to these acquired associates so you do need to manage the relationship carefully. Remember the malicious associate. It wouldn't be the first time an associate has left and taken their patient base with them when they felt they were getting a raw deal with the new owner!

If you find yourself in a similar situation, with associates already "in situ" in your new practice, then naturally, common sense tells us there will be a period of time when you will not want to rock the boat. The challenge, then, is trying to reconcile Michael's excellent ideas on The People Law, and the management of associates, and applying it to a setting where more often than not, you did not take on the associates in the first place! Though it is undoubtedly a difficult task, it is not an impossible one. If you've acquired, not hired, your associates, the secret then is to gradually introduce the E-Myth principles over time. Gradually let them see the light!

There is no doubt in our mind that managing associates is one of the biggest challenges of all. With a carefully thought out, diplomatic, and negotiated process, gradually you can persuade your associates that E-Myth will benefit everyone. After all, it's not about you making money. It's about making their lives better. It's about making happier patients, happier team members, happier associates, and ultimately, a happier you.

On that note, now seems the perfect time to see what Michael has to say on the subject of estimating. ❧

CHAPTER 13

On the Subject of Estimating

Michael E. Gerber

The best we can do is size up the chances, calculate the risks involved, estimate our ability to deal with them, and then make our plans with confidence.

—Henry Ford

One of the greatest weaknesses of dentists is accurately estimating how long appointments will take and then scheduling their patients accordingly. *Webster's Eleventh* defines estimate as "a rough or approximate calculation." Anyone who has visited a dentist's waiting room knows that those estimates can be rough indeed.

Do you want to see someone who gives you a rough approximation? What if your dentist gave you a rough approximation of your condition?

The fact is that we can predict many things we don't typically predict. For example, there are always ways to learn the truth about people who come in complaining about a toothache or in need of a root canal. Look at the steps of the process. Most of the things you do are standard, so develop a step-by-step system and stick to it.

In my book *The E-Myth Manager*, I raised eyebrows by suggesting that medical doctors eliminate the waiting room. Why? You don't need it if you're always on time. The same goes for a dental practice. If you're always on time, then your patients don't have to wait.

What if a dentist made this promise: on time, every time, as promised, or we pay for it.

"Impossible!" dentists cry. "Each patient is different. We simply can't know how long each appointment will take."

Do you follow this? Since dentists believe they're incapable of knowing how to organize their time, they build a practice based on lack of knowing and lack of control. They build a practice based on estimates.

I once had a dentist ask me, "What happens when someone comes in for a routine cleaning and we discover the state of their teeth is abysmal? How can we deal with someone so unexpected? How can we give proper care and stay on schedule?"

My first thought was that it's not being dealt with now. Few dentists are able to give generously of their time. Ask anyone who's been to a dentist's office lately. It's chaos.

The solution is interest, attention, analysis. Try detailing what you do at the beginning of an interaction, what you do in the middle, and what you do at the end. How long does each take? In the absence of such detailed, quantified standards, everything ends up being an estimate, and a poor estimate at that.

However, a practice organized around a system, with adequate staff to run it, has time for proper attention. It's built right into the system.

Too many dentists have grown accustomed to thinking in terms of estimates without thinking about what the term really means. Is it any wonder many dental practices are in trouble?

Enlightened dentists, in contrast, banish the word *estimate* from their vocabulary. When it comes to estimating, just say no!

"But you can never be exact," dentists have told me for years. "Close, maybe. But never exact."

I have a simple answer to that: *You have to be.* You simply can't afford to be inexact. You can't accept inexactness in yourself or in your dental practice.

You can't go to work every day believing that your practice, the work you do, and the commitments you make are all too complex and unpredictable to be exact. With a mindset like that, you're doomed to run a sloppy ship. A ship that will eventually sink and suck you down with it.

This is so easy to avoid. Sloppiness—in both thought and action—is the root cause of your frustrations.

The solution to those frustrations is clarity. Clarity gives you the ability to set a clear direction, which fuels the momentum you need to grow your business.

Clarity, direction, momentum—they all come from insisting on exactness.

But how do you create exactness in a hopelessly inexact world? The answer is this. You discover the exactness in your practice by refusing to do any work that can't be controlled exactly.

The only other option is to analyze the market, determine where the opportunities are, and then organize your practice to be the exact provider of the services you've chosen to offer.

Two choices, and only two choices: (1) evaluate your practice and then limit yourself to the tasks you know you can do exactly, or (2) start all over by analyzing the market, identifying the key opportunities in that market, and building a practice that operates exactly.

What you cannot do, what you must refuse to do, from this day forward, is to allow yourself to operate with an inexact mindset. It will lead you to ruin.

Which leads us inexorably back to the word I have been using through this book: *systems*.

Who makes estimates? Only dentists who are unclear about exactly how to do the task in question. Only dentists whose experience has taught them that if something can go wrong, it will—and to them!

I'm not suggesting that a *systems solution* will guarantee that you always perform exactly as promised. But I am saying that a systems solution will faithfully alert you when you're going off track, and will do it before you have to pay the price for it.

In short, with a systems solution in place, your need to estimate will be a thing of the past, both because you have organized your practice to anticipate mistakes, and because you have put into place the system to do something about those mistakes before they blow up.

There's this, too: To make a promise you intend to keep places a burden on you and your managers to dig deeply into how you intend to keep it. Such a burden will transform your intentions and increase your attention to detail.

With the promise will come dedication. With dedication will come integrity. With integrity will come consistency. With consistency will come results you can count on. And results you can count on mean that you get exactly what you hoped for at the outset of your practice: the true pride of ownership that every dentist should experience.

This brings us to the subject of *patients*. Who are they? Why do they come to you? How can you identify yours? And who *should* your patients be? But first, let's see what Al and Chris have to say about estimating. ❧

CHAPTER 14

Estimating

Dr. Alan Kwong Hing
Christopher Barrow

Opportunity, sooner or later, comes to all who work and wish.

—Lord Stanley

It has often been said that the best things in life are fees. Not only are they payment for your services, but they are also reward for your skill as a practitioner and the quality of treatment and care that you are able to provide. The scale of your fees is tied in very closely with your practice brand and the product you are selling to your patients. Just as with any other good or service, if patients perceive that they are receiving a better quality treatment, or a higher standard of care, then very often they will be willing to spend more on your services.

However, there is one proviso, and it's a big one: not every patient can afford high-end treatment. As we discussed in previous chapters, dentistry is in a unique position when compared to other healthcare providers in that people don't just come to you to relieve their toothache! A few years ago, if you wanted to see a dentist you could look up your nearest practice and be certain that whichever practice you went to, they would be able to meet your needs. Nowadays, however, dentistry has become more focused, and consumer power has meant that dental practices must now target themselves to a specific group of patients. If you want to be successful in modern dentistry, you will have to focus your efforts, too. Only once you have reflected on yourself, come up with a plan, and created the necessary systems that Michael talks about will you be in a position where you can best manage your time and your fees.

It's Time to Talk Fees

Another interesting part of the fees equation, globally, is that very often the fees you charge will be influenced by the jurisdiction or area that you practice in. In some countries for example, insurance is a major part of healthcare, and a suggested fee guide will be produced in consultation with insurance companies and dental associations. These fees are then a reflection of the time it takes you to deliver the service, the skills you require and the cost of the materials you use. Some jurisdictions will even go so far as to ask a sample of local dentists for their financial reports in order to find out what the overhead costs to practice are in the area, and make adjustments to fee recommendations accordingly.

This *guideline*, however, can in some cases become a *schedule*, as insurance companies will reimburse patients based on this guide. In certain circumstances we have known dentists who have become subject to discipline when the patient or the association has deemed their fees too high above what is usual and customarily charged by their colleagues, so sometimes you have to bear in mind that what you charge isn't always necessarily just down to you.

It's Time to Be Honest with Yourself

Aside from the murky topic of fees, one of the most common mistakes that many dentists make in estimating is they fail to effectively "zone" their appointment diary. As a dentist, and as a business owner, you need to recognize that there are many different types of dental activity—some more profitable than others. These zones of time can be divided into times when you are treating emergencies, time when you are dealing with long-term care and maintenance, and time when you are delivering more complex treatment.

The general rule of thumb is that the more complex and involved a treatment, the more expensive it is, and the higher the profit margins. So ideally, you want to be moving towards the more complex clinical end, as that's where the profit is. Unfortunately, things aren't always that simple. For a start, every dentist is different, and you probably have very different clinical interests to many colleagues in your local area. It may also be the case that you're not so comfortable doing complex treatments, and would much prefer to focus on long-term care. While choosing to follow this route is undoubtedly a very worthy cause, it's ultimately not where the money is at. If you do find that long-term care is where your passion lies, then you will need to consider other ways in which you can bring in extra revenues.

One of the best pieces of advice we can give you here is be honest with yourself. Every dentist is different and the term "dentistry" can mean many different things to many different people. Look at yourself in the mirror and ask yourself some important questions. Where are you clinically? How do you rate your clinical skills? What are your interests? What sort of practice do you want to run? Michael will talk about the subject of patients in the next chapter, but for now ask yourself: What sort of patients do you want to attract? Your skill, experience and motivations will lead you down certain paths, and as such, this may mean bringing in other dentists to cover the gaps in your own skill set.

As business owner it's down to you to take what you're good at and plan around it. If you find you're a "dabbler"—you dabble in implants, or you dabble in root canal treatments—then you need to face the reality that by dabbling and not focusing your efforts, you're never going to reach a level sufficient enough to be able to offer these treatments at a high enough standard. You will also find that you have lots of expensive specialist equipment lying around that simply isn't getting used!

Strangely enough, many dentists have not yet made the connection that the fees they charge ultimately lead to the income they will make, and that this income will dictate what their lifestyle will be. If you are satisfied with the simpler things in life, then doing simpler dental procedures with lower fees may be ok. If you would like a lot of bright, shiny, expensive objects, then you need to realize that placing fillings at say $200 an hour is a lot different from placing implants at, say, $1,000 an hour. So, if you have the skills and the inclination to do the higher fee-generating procedures, then there will be a corresponding higher level of income available for your lifestyle. Either way, the decision is completely up to you.

New Lead Generation

So you've decided what you're going to do, you have the practice and team with which to do it, but now what? Well now it's time to attract patients! One of the areas of dentistry in which it's very easy to become unprofitable is in providing consultations for prospective new patients. If your conversion rate for potential patients into *actual* patients is low, then you have to invest a lot of time into actually getting a result and building your book.

The problem here is that it's quite common for prospective new patients not to want to pay an awful lot of money for an initial consultation. Now, as a dentist you might want to target an average hourly rate for treatment at say $300–$400 per hour. But if you're targeting specifically new patients then you have a Catch-22 situation where if you want to spend a lot of time to get to know the patient and sell them the concept of your brand, then you're going to have to accept a major loss on that figure of $300–$400. Just imagine how many patients you'd attract if you put a figure of $300 for an initial consultation! Not many, that's for sure. It's only natural that patients should expect initial consultations to cost less. To balance out this problem, the natural solution would be to reduce the amount of time you spend in the initial consultation, but then, the less time you spend, the less likely you are to persuade the patient to join your practice. A real Catch-22!

Introducing the Treatment Coordinator

In response to the many difficulties associated with balancing time and money, one solution that's becoming increasingly popular is to employ a treatment coordinator. Very often this can be someone with dental nursing training who understands the language of dentistry and can then engage patients in conversations about their treatment and give them the time they deserve.

From a business perspective, employing a treatment coordinator is a far more effective use of practice time. If you have a treatment coordinator on your books, then this means you don't necessarily have to spend an hour, or however long with the patient—you don't need to be present for the entire time. Your treatment coordinator can also work on things such as building rapport, answering concerns, outlining treatment objectives, and so on, so you can focus more on doing dentistry and bringing in money to keep the practice running. It is important to note that you only earn as a dentist when you are actually doing a procedure, unless you have a practice where patients will accept paying you your regular hourly fee for a consultation. That is why the non-paying talking aspects can be completed by a well-trained treatment co-ordinator who will often do a much better job of educating you than they are spending the time with the patient so no question is left unanswered.

By employing a treatment coordinator you are making the decisive step towards working *on* the business as opposed to working *in* the business, which is one of Michael's primary goals for all small business owners to achieve. The treatment coordinator role makes the practice and patient relationships not all about you. Let's face it—if you're like most dentists out there, you struggle to speak to your patients about fees. Why? Because dental school has brainwashed you into thinking you cannot charge a lot of money for anything you do in dentistry! The use of a treatment coordinator, however, will help you overcome many problems you may have in explaining, and indeed justifying, your fees. As a result of a good patient educational process, the patient will understand their problem, the possible solutions available, and the fees involved, and will make a choice that fits their budget and their needs.

Striking a Balance

While employing a treatment coordinator is certainly a major advantage, this is not to say that without one, your practice won't succeed. The key thing here is to reflect, to plan, and to put systems in place that will make your practice a more effective, more efficient place of work.

In terms of putting the right systems in place, it's important you remember the importance of planning and good management. A big problem that many dentists encounter when it comes to estimating is that very often, they try and fit time to their patients' needs. As such, they end up forever chasing their own tails. Remember it's the dentists who fit the *patients to the time* that generally have the happier life!

It's also worth making a point here about treatment planning. If you're going to sell yourself effectively to your patients then they need to understand what it is you're offering, and why it is they need it. You need to be able to fully justify your fees.

You should recognize here that sometimes you will need to spend a little longer thinking about a treatment plan, and can't always provide a snap judgement for a patient on what their needs are and what the fees involved will be. It is far better to inform the patient that you will need time to do a proper analysis of their problem by examining x-rays, photographs, and models in detail, as this will allow you to come up with an accurate diagnosis while also producing several good, feasible treatment plan choices. Only then will the patient receive a full picture of what their situation is and what they can do about it, which will ultimately help them accept the fees that are being charged.

And here's another important point to remember: cut out the jargon! As a patient, if all you see on a treatment plan is "Crown on LR6" followed by a big number under the heading of cost, that means very little, and as a consumer your mind is in the setting where you are going to assess the value of that treatment based solely on the size of the number you have been quoted. You will naturally then be tempted to think you can get a better deal somewhere else! The more modern approach is to create a narrative that tells a story; for example, this is the problem, this is the effect the problem is having on your life, this is the solution we propose, and this is the benefit of the solution. The ability to turn the whole treatment planning process into a very personalized experience will serve you very well. Michael is right when he talks about systems for estimating and the need to insist on exactness in all you do.

Earlier we alluded to the fact that your fees will in some respects be determined by what the norm is for your area. In short, you have to become aware of what you do, how you do it, and who your patients are. The better you are, and the better your systems, the better your results will ultimately be. On that note, it seems a good place to pause and see what Michael has to say on the subject of patients. ♣

CHAPTER 15

On the Subject
of Patients

Michael E. Gerber

I don't build in order to have clients. I have clients in order to build.
—Ayn Rand

When it comes to the business of dentistry, the best definition of clients I've ever heard is this:
     Patients: *very special people who drive most dentists crazy.*
Does that work for you?

After all, it's a rare patient who shows any appreciation for what a
dentist has to go through to do the job as promised. Don't they always
think the price is too high? And don't they focus on problems, broken
promises, and the mistakes they think you make, rather than all the
ways you bend over backward to give them what they need?

Do you ever hear other dentists voice these complaints? More
to the point, have you ever voiced them yourself? Well, you're not
alone. I have yet to meet a dentist who doesn't suffer from a strong
case of patient confusion.

Patient confusion is about:

- what your patient really wants;
- how to communicate effectively with your patient;
- how to keep your patient happy;
- how to deal with patient dissatisfaction; and
- whom to call a patient.

Confusion 1: What Your Patient Really Wants

Your patients aren't just people; they're very specific kinds of people. Let me share with you the six categories of patients as seen from the E-Myth marketing perspective: (1) tactile patients, (2) neutral patients, (3) withdrawal patients, (4) experimental patients, (5) transitional patients, and (6) traditional patients.

Your entire marketing strategy must be based on which type of patient you are dealing with. Each of the six patient types spends money on dental services for very different, and identifiable, reasons. These are:

- Tactile patients get their major gratification from interacting with other people.
- Neutral patients get their major gratification from interacting with inanimate objects (computers, cars, information).
- Withdrawal patients get their major gratification from interacting with ideas (thoughts, concepts, stories).
- Experimental patients rationalize their buying decisions by perceiving that what they bought is new, revolutionary, and innovative.
- Transitional patients rationalize their buying decisions by perceiving that what they bought is dependable and reliable.
- Traditional patients rationalize their buying decisions by perceiving that what they bought is cost-effective, a good deal, and worth the money.

In short:

- If your patient is tactile, you have to emphasize the *people* of your practice.
- If your patient is neutral, you have to emphasize the *technology* of your practice.
- If your patient is a withdrawal patient, you have to emphasize the *idea* of your practice.
- If your patient is experimental, you have to emphasize the *uniqueness* of your practice.
- If your patient is transitional, you have to emphasize the *dependability* of your practice.
- If your patient is traditional, you have to talk about the *financial competitiveness* of your practice.

What your patients want is determined by who they are. Who they are is regularly demonstrated by what they do. Think about the patients with whom you do business. Ask yourself: In which of the categories would I place them? What do they do for a living?

If your patient is a mechanical engineer, for example, it's probably safe to assume he's a neutral patient. If another one of your patients is a cardiologist, she's probably tactile. Accountants tend to be traditional, and software engineers are often experimental.

Having an idea about which categories your patients may fall into is very helpful to figuring out what they want. Of course, there's no exact science to it, and human beings constantly defy stereotypes. So don't take my word for it. You'll want to make your own analysis of the patients you serve.

Confusion 2: How to Communicate Effectively with Your Patient

The next step in the patient satisfaction process is to decide how to magnify the characteristics of your practice that are most likely to appeal to your preferred category of patient. That begins with what marketing people call your *positioning strategy*.

What do I mean by *positioning* your practice? You position your practice with words. A few well-chosen words to tell your patients exactly what they want to hear. In marketing lingo, those words are called your USP, or unique selling proposition.

For example, if you are targeting tactile patients (ones who love people), your USP could be: "Wellness Care, where the feelings of people *really* count!"

If you are targeting experimental patients (ones who love new, revolutionary things), your USP could be: "Wellness Care, where living on the edge is a way of life!" In other words, when they choose to schedule an appointment with you, they can count on both your services and equipment to be on the cutting edge of the dental industry.

Is this starting to make sense? Do you see how the ordinary things most dentists do to get patients can be done in a significantly more effective way?

Once you understand the essential principles of marketing the E-Myth way, the strategies by which you attract patients can make an enormous difference in your market share.

Confusion 3: How to Keep Your Patient Happy

Let's say you've overcome the first two confusions. Great. Now how do you keep your patient happy?

Very simple . . . just keep your promise! And make sure your patient *knows* you kept your promise every step of the way.

In short, giving your patients what they think they want is the key to keeping your patients (or anyone else, for that matter) really happy.

If your patients need to interact with people (high touch, tactile), make certain that they do.

If they need to interact with things (high-tech, neutral), make certain that they do.

If they need to interact with ideas (in their head, withdrawal), make certain that they do.

And so forth.

At E-Myth, we call this your *patient fulfillment system*. It's the step-by-step process by which you do the task you've contracted to do and deliver what you've promised—on time, every time.

But what happens when your patients are *not* happy? What happens when you've done everything I've mentioned here and your patient is still dissatisfied?

Confusion 4: How to Deal with Patient Dissatisfaction

If you have followed each step up to this point, patient dissatisfaction will be rare. But it can and will still occur—people are people, and some people will always find a way to be dissatisfied with something. Here's what to do about it:

- Always listen to what your patients are saying. And never interrupt while they're saying it.
- After you're sure you've heard all of your patient's complaint, make absolutely certain you understand what she said by phrasing a question, such as: "Can I repeat what you've just told me, Ms. Harton, to make absolutely certain I understand you?"
- Secure your patient's acknowledgment that you have heard her complaint accurately.
- Apologize for whatever your patient thinks you did that dissatisfied her, even if you didn't do it!
- After your patient has acknowledged your apology, ask her exactly what would make her happy.
- Repeat what your patient told you would make her happy, and get her acknowledgment that you have heard correctly.
- If at all possible, give your patient exactly what she has asked for.

You may be thinking, "But what if my patient wants something totally impossible?" Don't worry. If you've followed my recommendations to the letter, what your patient asks for will seldom seem unreasonable.

Confusion 5: Whom to Call a Patient

At this stage, it's important to ask yourself some questions about the kind of patients you hope to attract to your company:

- Which types of patients would you most like to do business with?
- Where do you see your real market opportunities?
- Who would you like to work with, provide services to, and position your business for?

In short, *it's all up to you.* No mystery. No magic. Just a systematic process for shaping your practice's future. But you must have the passion to pursue the process. And you must be absolutely clear about every aspect of it.

Until you know your patients as well as you know yourself.

Until all your complaints about patients are a thing of the past.

Until you accept the undeniable fact that patient acquisition and patient satisfaction are more science than art.

But unless you're willing to grow your practice, you'd better not follow any of these recommendations. Because if you do what I'm suggesting, it's going to grow.

This brings us to the subject of *growth*. But first, let's see what Al and Chris have to say about patients. ❧

CHAPTER 16

Your Patients and You

Dr. Alan Kwong Hing
Christopher Barrow

Charity, good behavior, amiable speech, unselfishness—these by the chief sage have been declared the elements of popularity.

—Burmese Proverb

As a dentist, patients are at the heart of everything you do. Patients can be difficult sometimes, but it's your job as business owner to confront what Michael calls "patient confusion." It's only by knowing who your patients are and what they want that they will be fully satisfied with the service and return to your practice time and time again.

Who Are Your Patients?

It may seem like a strange question, but it really is fundamental to understanding the E-Myth philosophy. Once you fully understand precisely *who* your patients are, you will then be better placed to ascertain their needs and so give them what they want.

A few decades ago, the definition of a patient was anybody and everybody, but nowadays there's very much an emphasis on focussing care to a specific market or demographic.

This change has come about from the recognition that if you're in an urban regeneration area for example, your patients are going to have very different requirements than perhaps those attending a spa practice in an affluent part of a major city. What's happening now is dental practices are being designed, and the teams within them are being employed, to appeal very specifically to a certain type of patient. We're moving away from the scenario twenty years ago where a dental practice was a place where anyone could turn up with any problem and have that problem solved. Those general practices still exist, but they're very much in the decline.

You Get to Choose!

One of the most liberating aspects of Michael's E-Myth philosophy is that it reminds us that as a business owner, you get to choose the sorts of patients you want to attract. This is because you choose the practice, the location, the staff and the treatments, and based on these decisions, you will attract a certain type of patient.

This all links back very closely to our earlier discussion on the subject of planning, and it is important very early on that you choose precisely the type of patients you want your practice to attract, and so build your working environment, your team, and your systems around that target market.

In the previous chapter on estimating, we spoke about how the treatment you want to deliver and the fees you want to charge can impact on your earnings and lifestyle. These decisions also make it imperative that you choose the right type of patients who need what you want to deliver, have them understand what is involved in the treatment, and can afford to pay the fees for the services that you want to provide.

So in essence, it's all about targeting your efforts effectively. If you've got an older demographic, you're not going to want a young, hip, and trendy looking practice, or one that looks like a minimalist airport lounge. The aim here is to create physical environments that are demographically tailored to a specific group of patients. The same applies to the sorts of team members you employ. Certain demographics, for example, prefer certain sorts of staff members. A young demographic might not be so happy with a very old, very stern receptionist who isn't so "young-people friendly."

The Art of Good Communication

As Michael states in his six categories of patients, having you and your team aware of what category different patients fit into should be reviewed regularly and all members of the team should be communicating with the patient in the method that suits them best.

The use of patient educational tools that are available will also help your patients understand what is happening. Too often dentists forget that patients aren't as in touch with dentistry as they are. If you hold up a small x-ray to a patient and ask them if they can see the cavity, how many will really understand what you are showing them? Unless they are a dentist themselves, the chances are they won't!

Now imagine the difference if the small x-ray slide was blown up on a widescreen monitor and the cavity highlighted by a 3-D image. Personally, we love advocating the use of patient education models, as it is better to have the patient feel how hard it is to remove a denture secured by implants than trying to explain it in words. A well-animated video of two minutes that explains the process of root canal treatment can be much more informative and beneficial to the patient than your own explanation.

Other steps you can take include producing information booklets on the different treatments you carry out. A well-designed booklet that illustrates the steps in having a crown instead of a large filling on a tooth can be taken home for the patient to review. Your website can also be a useful tool here. By posting a number of good patient testimonials under each specific procedure you offer, you can help patients understand that they are not the only ones who have a certain problem, and that there are solutions out there that other people are happy with.

Knowing what category your patient fits into and tailoring your patient education material only enhances the whole process so your patient doesn't suffer from a case of confusion.

Other Things to Consider

Following on from your choice of location, building, and team, you should also aim to tailor your marketing systems around the type of patients you want to attract. The same applies to your customer service systems. Would your target group prefer to receive appointment reminders by text message or by telephone call? Would they prefer to receive a letter or an email?

The customer service system built around confirming patients for their appointments should also be considered an opportunity to lessen patient confusion. If a phone call is made to confirm an appointment, the message should not be, "I am calling to confirm your appointment at 11:30 a.m. tomorrow." Rather, it should be, "Hello Mrs. Jones, this is Laura from the Grand River Dental Office, and I am calling to confirm your 11:30 a.m. root canal appointment tomorrow, which will be finished at 12:30 p.m. We have prescribed you antibiotics prior to the appointment, so please take them as directed and feel free to contact me at 123-456-7891, or visit our website for further information."

Finally, you should also consider your choice of dentist. If you're dealing with a lot of people over fifty, then you know you will be doing a lot of advanced work and you will need to employ associates who are comfortable with doing that sort of work. Similarly, if you're dealing with people under the age of thirty-five, the work you carry out will typically be of a simpler nature as many of the patients from this demographic do not require significant complex dental care since they have benefitted from fluoride and regular preventive dental care.

So, right at the beginning of your project you need to say to yourself, "I want to work in a practice that looks like X, with people like Y who act like Z." You need to very firmly establish what it is you want, and then plan sufficiently to put in place the systems and procedures to help you bring about that aim.

Keeping Your Patients Happy

Once you've set up your practice and you've attracted your patients, the next thing you need to really focus your efforts on is how to keep your patients happy.

In the last chapter, Michael makes some excellent points on patient communication. As a dentist, and also as a business owner, you need to recognize that different people communicate differently, and as such some patients will require a different communicative approach to others. At the heart of Michael's message, however, is this whole notion of managing expectations.

In our mind, openness is key. When a patient first visits your practice, it's important that you recognize that in a patient's first visit, your role is to introduce them to your brand. In that first meeting, an exchange of expectations also takes place between you and the patient. You outline to the patient what they can expect to receive in terms of care and treatment, and in turn the patient is informed of their duties to you (punctuality and so forth). It is interesting to note that patients' charters are becoming more and more common here—not just in dentistry, but in other healthcare professions as well. Whether you adopt such a step is, of course, completely up to you, but you need to remember in that first meeting you set the tone for what is to follow—you set the standard for the values that your practice represents.

When it comes to planning and actually carrying out treatments, again, good communication is essential. Time and time again the secret here is to manage the expectations of whomever you are treating. When you are completing a treatment plan, discuss your patient's expectations with them. Head off any surprises before they crop up. Pain, function, time, and cost are four major areas where patients may find that their expectations are challenged, so it's your role to explain precisely what the procedure is, why it is necessary, the benefits it will bring, and so on.

In an attempt to keep the patient happy, it also helps the patient who has multiple appointments to track the process with them. Thus, by providing them with a plan complete with timeframes, and periodically checking in with them to confirm progress, the result will be a happy patient who will not be dissatisfied with the treatment and will feel value for the fees they are paying. After all, you can never be at fault for giving too much clear information, but can definitely run into issues if you have not provided enough.

The more effort you put in here at the treatment planning stage, the more likely your patients are to be completely satisfied with the treatment they have received. A little effort really can go a long way!

A Footnote on Recordkeeping

On the subject of patients and patient communication, it is worthwhile pausing for a moment here to consider the very important issue of records. We live in a world now where recordkeeping is paramount, and good recordkeeping can potentially save you from litigation. Though by following the E-Myth principles, carefully managing your patients, and developing systems, you will be far less likely to encounter problems. Experience tells us that sometimes, despite all your best efforts, things just don't work out. To cover your back, in case anything should go wrong (though we hope it never does), we strongly recommend that everything you say and do, and everything your patients say and do, should be recorded and signed off as being recorded.

The same goes for recordkeeping done by your staff, from the person working on the front desk who takes a call from a patient to cancel their appointment, to the hygienist who has spoken to a patient about why a broken tooth would benefit from a crown. Any and all things said to a patient or said by a patient should be noted. Many times, dentists will discuss a procedure with a patient and leave the room. The patient then turns to the assistant and asks, "What was that again?" As the conversation with the assistant has clarified the situation, this should also be noted in the chart. This is all a part of the patient fulfilment system, as the assistant will then reconnect with the dentist or treatment coordinator and address the patient's questions and concerns. Together then, as a team, the treatment can be delivered so that the patient is completely satisfied and happy with the treatment they receive.

So, there you have it, another piece in the puzzle. Hopefully things are looking a lot clearer for you now the full picture is starting to take shape. Now let's get the next piece of the puzzle from Michael, as he talks about growth. ✤

CHAPTER 17

On the Subject of Growth

Michael E. Gerber

*As we learn we always change, and so our perception. This changed
perception then becomes a new Teacher inside each of us.*

—Hyemeyohsts Storm

The rule of business growth says that every business, like every
child, is destined to grow. Needs to grow. Is determined to grow.

Once you've created your dental practice, once you've
shaped the idea of it, the most natural thing for it to do is to . . . *grow!*
And if you stop it from growing, it will die.

Once a dentist has started a practice, it's his or her job to help
it grow. To nurture it and support it in every way. To infuse it with

- Purpose;
- Passion;
- Will;
- Belief;

- Personality; and
- Method.

As your practice grows, it naturally changes. And as it changes from a small practice to something much bigger, you will begin to feel out of control. News flash: that's because you *are* out of control.

Your practice *has* exceeded your know-how, sprinted right past you, and now it's taunting you to keep up. That leaves you two choices: grow as big as your practice demands you grow, or try to hold your practice at its present level—at the level you feel most comfortable.

The sad fact is that most dentists do the latter. They try to keep their practice small, securely within their comfort zone. Doing what they know how to do, what they feel most comfortable doing. It's called playing it safe.

But as the practice grows, the number, scale, and complexity of tasks will grow, too, until they threaten to overwhelm the dentist. More people are needed. More space. More money. Everything seems to be happening at the same time. A hundred balls are in the air at once.

As I've said throughout this book: Most dentists are not entrepreneurs. They aren't true businesspeople at all, but technicians suffering from an entrepreneurial seizure. Their philosophy of coping with the workload can be summarized as "just do it," rather than figuring out how to get it done through other people using innovative systems to produce consistent results.

Given most dentist's inclination to be the master juggler in their practice, it's not surprising that as complexity increases, as work expands beyond their ability to do it, as money becomes more elusive, they are just holding on, desperately juggling more and more balls. In the end, most collapse under the strain.

You can't expect your practice to stand still. You can't expect your practice to stay small. A practice that stays small and depends on you to do everything isn't a practice—it's a job!

Yes, just like your children, your business must be allowed to grow, to flourish, to change, to become more than it is. In this way, it will match your vision. And you know all about vision, right? You'd better. It's what you do best!

Do you feel the excitement? You should. After all, you know what your practice *is* but not what it *can be*.

It's either going to grow or die. The choice is yours, but it is a choice that must be made. If you sit back and wait for change to overtake you, you will always have to answer no to this question: Are you ready?

This brings us to the subject of *change*. But first, let's see what Al and Chris have to say about growth. ❧

CHAPTER 18

Growth

Dr. Alan Kwong Hing
Christopher Barrow

If we're growing, we're always going to be out of our comfort zone
—John Maxwell

M ichael is absolutely right when he reminds us of the importance of growth. In a market that's continually growing, if your business shrinks, or even just fails to grow sufficiently, then your competitors will pull ahead and your business will start to die.

One of the main problems facing the dental profession today is that dental schools across the world try to instil a sense of pride and professionalism that tells you to be successful in dentistry you only need to be a good dentist. Witness, for example, the white coat ceremony that many faculties now have the incoming classes undertake, where they have to swear to uphold the tenets of the profession, and be good, ethical dentists.

What the professors don't tell you, of course, is that it's not just about being a good dentist! This is because, as we have seen, there is a clear disconnect between growing your practice and being a professional. You may be the best dentist in the world, but without good marketing and a well-thought-out, structured business plan, you won't be successful. After all, the patient does not know that you gave a perfectly contoured filling with all the accessory grooves on a molar. What they do know is that you did the procedure without any pain and that they did not spend a long time in the chair.

With this in mind, it's useful to take a step back for a moment and consider what it is you're doing as a business owner and precisely why you're doing it. Remember, as Michael says, the objective of any business is to make a profit. The purpose of a business is to solve someone else's problem and be well rewarded for the solution.

As the owner of a dental business then, it's your job to solve someone else's problem. While in some industries there may be many different problems that can be solved, in dentistry, there are fundamentally only two. One is function, and the other is appearance. Either you are working to make someone's teeth function properly and/or relieve them of pain, or you are working to improve the appearance of their teeth.

While the function market is undoubtedly a very important area of dentistry, the fact is people are far more prepared to spend money on appearance than function. For this reason, if you really want to see your business grow, you need to embrace the appearance market, and you can't just focus on function.

This dilemma of function vs. appearance is one that comes up time and time again in dentistry, and can be linked back with this idea of "professionalism" and "what it means to be a professional" that many of the professors teach young dentists when they first join dental school. It seems strange to us that in this day and age, many in the profession still frown upon cosmetic procedures such as smile makeovers, yet at the same time they would have no concern sending a patient to the orthodontist to have their teeth straightened.

Is there really that much of a difference between the two? Whereas in the past there would seem to be a clear argument against veneers and the more aggressive cosmetic treatments available, now in the twenty-first century, it is possible to have both form *and* function so there can really be no reason why you shouldn't offer treatments that will help your practice grow.

Needs vs. Wants

If we look more closely at the function and appearance markets, we see the classic split between "needs" and "wants." Though it's fair to say more people "need" functional treatment in dentistry as a whole, the smaller "wants" market is a far more profitable area to explore.

Across many regions of the world now, the market for functional dentistry has pretty well flat-lined and has been stagnant for a long time. A part of this is, of course, due to the economic downturn and government cutbacks, but it's also clear that there's no seasonal variation when it comes to function needs. Another reason behind this stagnation is that functional dentistry is being commoditized. To grow in a commodity world, then, the debate is about hourly and piecework vs. a results-oriented outcome. To work as a functionality-oriented dentist, there is a limit to the capacity you can grow as you can only drill and fill so many holes with attention to detail in one hour. Then it becomes a matter of how many you can do, and not how well. You then become a functional production line, and there is only so far you can grow before you either burn out or the quality of your work starts to decline.

But while the functional market has a number of quite powerful limitations on it, the appearance market is continuing to grow at an almost exponential rate. The most affluent demographic group in society is that of the over forty-five year olds. These people have moved through successive generations, and are now starting to reap the fruits of their labours—they are selling businesses, taking early retirement, inheriting property, finishing their children's education, and paying off mortgages. They're reaching a stage where they have the time and money to enjoy themselves, and so as part of this want to look and feel good.

This is a remarkably exciting opportunity for a dentist with the skills and the desire to take advantage of this ever-developing market. We have people who want treatment, and importantly, can pay for the sorts of treatments that they desire. The growth opportunity in this market then is far larger than it has been at any other time in dentistry. There are even people now getting into full mouth rehabilitation, where patients can go from having a set of upper and lower dentures to having a complete set of fixed teeth with implants in the space of a single day.

Technological advances such as these allow us to provide treatment faster and with better results than ever before. The range of treatments available has also expanded to include the likes of basic orthodontic appliances that can be provided by an average dentist without the need for specialist training. So the market for dental services has expanded dramatically and we have the ability to both attract and treat people who may not have had certain types of dentistry before because of their issues or concerns.

A lot of the product development in dentistry over the last few years has been fuelled by this expanding market, and this development has expanded the market further still in a continuing spiral of growth. What we've got then is more and more people with more and more money wanting more and more things from dentistry. And the great thing is, you're in a position to give it to them!

You've really got no choice but to take advantage of this. You are surfing a wave that's getting bigger and bigger every year. It's almost a situation where you can't not grow. Every year there are more products available to satisfy demand, and more people are showing up at practices with the money and the desire to improve their teeth.

It would be economically idiotic to miss out on this process. Even if you're operating a National Health practice and offering functional dentistry, as an independent practitioner you still have an obligation to grow your market share (even of a static market). If you don't, you will be committing economic suicide for your business. As Michael so rightly says, "If your business stops growing, then it will ultimately die."

Growth Begins with You!

Given the importance of growth and just how much opportunity is out there for the savvy dentist keen to expand their business, it's surprising just how many practices *still* don't do anything, and still don't take the opportunity to develop and grow their business. If this is you then remember, it's not too late! Take action now!

The first thing you need to look at here is yourself. Commit to learning about what is new and also what innovations have been done, even with functional or basic dental treatments. You may be surprised. The path to growth always starts with yourself, and you should devote yourself to a course of continuing education and growing both as a professional, and also as a person. Rather than having your licensing board push you into a minimum number of continuing education credits, commit to taking things into your own hands and getting more learning under your belt. You could even choose to enrol on a further education course, or take part in distance learning. Whatever you do, remember that a commitment to grow yourself will in turn lead to growth of your office. It's not wasted effort!

So how do you go about learning and growing then? The simplest answer here is to read the myriad of magazines that come to your practice each month. We're not saying everything is gospel, but read to learn and grow. Online education is still in its infancy, but there is still some outstanding material to be found online. Conferences are also a great way to meet up with colleagues and review what is new.

The most important thing here is that you need to embrace the fact that your growth as a dentist doesn't end when you leave dental school. It's a life-long journey and by growing yourself, the end result will be growth in your business. Then, one day, when you do finally get to retire, you will have grown an office you can sell for an amount that reflects your time and efforts to stay abreast of and grow within the profession.

Don't Forget Your Practice!

Once you've established a firm framework for your own personal growth and development, you can then apply a similar kind of framework to your own practice. Just as you'd review your own level of development on a regular basis, the same should really apply to your practice as well.

In our work offering business advice to practices, it's not unusual for us to walk into practices and find ourselves in facilities that are over fifteen years old—and you can really tell! Sometimes dentists in these practices will argue that, "Well, up until ten years ago, patients didn't care—when you have toothache, you don't care what the wallpaper looks like"

Ok, so maybe up until the 1990s this may have been the case, but things are different now. Times have changed—dentistry is now a super-competitive market. People are looking for confidence and improvement in appearance. Patients are savvy—they know that they can shop around.

Appearance of practice and level of reinvestment in the business are important. You have an obligation to grow as it sends the signal to patients that you are up to date. Even if you only invested in your practice four or five years ago, it's always worthwhile giving your practice a lick of paint every few years. After all, it shows your patients that you are committed to growth and moving your business forward. It also shows your patients that you care!

Does that make sense? Hopefully now things are starting to slot into place. On that note, now seems the perfect time to see what Michael has to say about the subject of change. ❧

CHAPTER 19

On the Subject
of Change

Michael E. Gerber

*The "rest of the world" does not sit idly "out there." It is a sparkling
realm of continual creation, transformation, and annihilation.*
        —Gary Zukav, *The Dancing Wu Li Masters*

S
o your practice is growing. That means, of course, that it's also
changing. Which means it's driving you and everyone in your
life crazy.

That's because, to most people, change is a diabolical thing. Tell
most people they've got to change, and their first instinct is to crawl
into a hole. Nothing threatens their existence more than change.
Nothing cements their resistance more than change. Nothing.

Yet for the past thirty-five years, that's exactly what I've been
proposing to small business owners: the need to change. Not for the
sake of change itself, but for the sake of their lives.

I've talked to countless dentists whose hopes weren't being realized through their practice; whose lives were consumed by work;

who slaved increasingly longer hours for decreasing pay; whose dissatisfaction grew as their enjoyment shriveled; whose practice had become the worst job in the world; whose money was out of control; whose employees were a source of never-ending hassles, just like their patients, their bank, and, increasingly, even their families.

More and more, these dentists spent their time alone, dreading the unknown and anxious about the future. And even when they were with people, they didn't know how to relax. Their mind was always on the job. They were distracted by work, by the thought of work. By the fear of falling behind.

And yet, when confronted with their condition and offered an alternative, most of the same dentists strenuously resisted. They assumed that if there were a better way of doing business, they already would have figured it out. They derived comfort from knowing what they believed they already knew. They accepted the limitations of being a dentist; or the truth about people; or the limitations of what they could expect from their patients, their employees, their associate dentists, their bankers—even their family and friends.

In short, most dentists I've met over the years would rather live with the frustrations they already have than risk enduring new frustrations.

Isn't that true of most people you know? Rather than opening up to the infinite number of possibilities life offers, they prefer to shut their life down to respectable limits. After all, isn't that the most reasonable way to live?

I think not. I think we must learn to let go. I think that if you fail to embrace change, it will inevitably destroy you.

Conversely, by opening yourself to change, you give your dental practice the opportunity to get the most from your talents.

Let me share with you an original way to think about change, about life, about who we are and what we do. About the stunning notion of expansion and contraction.

Contraction vs. Expansion

"Our salvation," a wise man once said, "is to allow." That is, to be open, to let go of our beliefs, to change. Only then can we move from a point of view to a viewing point.

That wise man was Thaddeus Golas, the author of a small, powerful book entitled *The Lazy Man's Guide to Enlightenment* (Seed Center, 1971).

Among the many inspirational things he had to say was this compelling idea:

> *The basic function of each being is expanding and contracting. Expanded beings are permeative; contracted beings are dense and impermeative. Therefore each of us, alone or in combination, may appear as space, energy, or mass, depending on the ratio of expansion to contraction chosen, and what kind of vibrations each of us expresses by alternating expansion and contraction. Each being controls his own vibrations.*

In other words, Golas tells us that the entire mystery of life can be summed up in two words: *expansion* and *contraction*. He goes on to say:

> *We experience expansion as awareness, comprehension, understanding, or whatever we wish to call it.*
>
> *When we are completely expanded, we have a feeling of total awareness, of being one with all life.*
>
> *At that level we have no resistance to any vibrations or interactions of other beings. It is timeless bliss, with unlimited choice of consciousness, perception, and feeling.*
>
> *When a [human] being is totally contracted, he is a mass particle, completely imploded.*
>
> *To the degree that he is contracted, a being is unable to be in the same space with others, so contraction is felt as fear, pain, unconsciousness, ignorance, hatred, evil, and a whole host of strange feelings.*
>
> *At an extreme [of contraction, a human being] has the feeling of being completely insane, of resisting everyone and everything, of being unable to choose the content of his consciousness.*

Of course, these are just the feelings appropriate to mass vibration levels, and he can get out of them at any time by expanding, by letting go of all resistance to what he thinks, sees, or feels.

Stay with me here. Because what Golas says is profoundly important. When you're feeling oppressed, overwhelmed, exhausted by more than you can control—contracted, as Golas puts it—you can change your state to one of expansion.

According to Golas, the more contracted we are, the more threatened by change; the more expanded we are, the more open to change.

In our most enlightened—that is, open—state, change is as welcome as non-change. Everything is perceived as a part of ourselves. There is no inside or outside. Everything is one thing. Our sense of isolation is transformed to a feeling of ease, of light, of joyful relationship with everything.

As infants, we didn't even think of change in the same way, because we lived those first days in an unthreatened state. Insensitive to the threat of loss, most young children are only aware of *what is*. Change is simply another form of *what is*. Change just *is*.

However, when we are in our most contracted—that is, closed—state, change is the most extreme threat. If the known is what I have, then the unknown must be what threatens to take away what I have. Change, then, is the unknown. And the unknown is fear. It's like being between trapezes.

- To the fearful, change is threatening because things may get worse.
- To the hopeful, change is encouraging because things may get better.
- To the confident, change is inspiring because the challenge exists to improve things.

If you are fearful, you see difficulties in every opportunity. If you are fear-free, you see opportunities in every difficulty.

Fear protects what I have from being taken away. But it also disconnects me from the rest of the world. In other words, fear keeps me separate and alone.

Here's the exciting part of Golas's message: with this new under-standing of contraction and expansion, we can become completely attuned to where we are at all times.

If I am afraid, suspicious, skeptical, and resistant, I am in a contracted state. If I am joyful, open, interested, and willing, I am in an expanded state. Just knowing this puts me on an expanded path. Always remembering this, Golas says, brings enlightenment, which opens me even more.

Such openness gives me the ability to freely access my options. And taking advantage of options is the best part of change. Just as there are infinite ways to greet a client, there are infinite ways to run your company. If you believe Thaddeus Golas, your most exciting option is to be open to all of them.

Because your life is lived on a continuum between the most contracted and most expanded—the most closed and most open—states, change is best understood as the movement from one to the other, and back again.

Most small-business owners I've met see change as a thing in itself, as something that just happens to them. Most experience change as a threat. Whenever change shows up at the door, they quickly slam it. Many bolt the door and pile up the furniture. Some even run for their gun.

Few of them understand that change isn't a thing in itself, but rather the manifestation of many things. You might call it the revela-tion of all possibilities. Think of it as the ability at any moment to sacrifice what we are for what we could become.

Change can either challenge us or threaten us. It's our choice. Our attitude toward change can either pave the way to success or throw up a roadblock.

Change is where opportunity lives. Without change we would stay exactly as we are. The universe would be frozen still. Time would end.

At any given moment, we are somewhere on the path between a contracted and expanded state. Most of us are in the middle of the journey, neither totally closed nor totally open. According to Golas, change is our movement from one place in the middle toward one of the two ends.

Do you want to move toward contraction or toward enlightenment? Because without change, you are hopelessly stuck with what you've got.

Without change,

- we have no hope;
- we cannot know true joy;
- we will not get better; and
- we will continue to focus exclusively on what we have and the threat of losing it.

All of this negativity contracts us even more, until, at the extreme closed end of the spectrum, we become a black hole so dense that no light can get in or out.

Sadly, the harder we try to hold on to what we've got, the less able we are to do so. So we try still harder, which eventually drags us even deeper into the black hole of contraction.

Are you like that? Do you know anybody who is?

Think of change as the movement between where we are and where we're not. That leaves only two directions for change: either moving forward or slipping backward. We become either more contracted or more expanded.

The next step is to link change to how we feel. If we feel afraid, change is dragging us backward. If we feel open, change is pushing us forward.

Change is not a thing in itself, but a movement of our consciousness. By tuning in, by paying attention, we get clues to the state of our being.

Change, then, is not an outcome or something to be acquired. Change is a shift of our consciousness, of our being, of our humanity, of our attention, of our relationship with all other beings in the universe.

We are either "more in relationship" or "less in relationship." Change is the movement in either of those directions. The exciting part is that *we possess the ability to decide which way we go . . . and to know, in the moment, which way we're moving.*

Closed, open . . . Open, closed. Two directions in the universe. The choice is yours.

Do you see the profound opportunity available to you? What an extraordinary way to live!

Enlightenment is not reserved for the sainted. Rather, it comes to us as we become more sensitive to ourselves. Eventually, we become our own guides, alerting ourselves to our state, moment by moment: *open . . . closed . . . open . . . closed.*

Listen to your inner voice, your ally, and feel what it's like to be open and closed. Experience the instant of choice in both directions.

You will feel the awareness growing. It may be only a flash at first, so be alert. This feeling is accessible, but only if you avoid the black hole of contraction.

Are you afraid that you're totally contracted? Don't be—it's doubtful. The fact that you're still reading this book suggests that you're moving in the opposite direction.

You're more like a running back seeking the open field. You can see the opportunity gleaming in the distance. In the open direction.

Understand that I'm not saying that change itself is a point on the path; rather, it's the all-important movement.

Change is *in you*, not *out there*.

What path are you on? The path of liberation? Or the path of crystallization?

As we know, change can be for the better or for the worse.

If change is happening *inside* of you, it is for the worse only if you remain closed to it. The key, then, is your attitude—your acceptance or rejection of change. Change can be for the better only if you accept it. And it will certainly be for the worse if you don't.

Remember, change is nothing in itself. Without you, change doesn't exist. Change is happening inside of each of us, giving us clues to where we are at any point in time.

Rejoice in change, for it's a sign you are alive.

Are we open? Are we closed? If we're open, good things are bound to happen. If we're closed, things will only get worse.

According to Golas, it's as simple as that. Whatever happens defines where we are. *How* we are is *where* we are. It cannot be any other way.

For change is life.

Charles Darwin wrote, "It is not the strongest of the species that survive, nor the most intelligent, but the one that proves itself most responsive to change."

The growth of your dental practice, then, is its change. Your role is to go with it, to be with it, to share the joy, embrace the opportunities, meet the challenges, learn the lessons.

Remember, there are three kinds of people: (1) those who make things happen, (2) those who let things happen, and (3) those who wonder what the hell happened. The people who make things happen are masters of change. The other two are its victims.

Which type are you?

The Big Change

If all this is going to mean anything to the life of your practice, you have to know when you're going to leave it. At what point, in your practice's rise from where it is now to where it can ultimately grow, are you going to sell it? Because if you don't have a clear picture of when you want out, your practice is the master of your destiny, not the reverse.

As we stated earlier, the most valuable form of money is equity, and unless your business vision includes your equity and how you will use it to your advantage, you will forever be consumed by your practice.

Your practice is potentially the best friend you ever had. It is your practice's nature to serve you, so let it. If, however, you are not a wise steward, if you do not tell your practice what you expect from it, it will run rampant, abuse you, use you, and confuse you.

Change. Growth. Equity.

Focus on the point in the future when you will take leave of your practice. Now reconsider your goals in that context. Be specific. Write them down.

Skipping this step is like tiptoeing through earthquake country. Who can say where the fault lies waiting? And who knows exactly when your whole world may come crashing down around you?

Which brings us to the subject of *time*. But first, let's see what Al and Chris have to say about change. ❧

CHAPTER 20

Embrace the Change!

Dr. Alan Kwong Hing
Christopher Barrow

Be the change that you wish to see in the world.

—Gandhi

I f your business is going to become the best it can be, then it isn't just going to grow, but it's also going to change. When your business grows, change will come whether you want it to or not. You'd only be fooling yourself if you don't want anything to change in your workplace, as the world is a constantly changing place.

Take your staff for example. As time goes by, changes might occur in their personal lives, which may change the way they approach their work. And even work itself is constantly in a state of change. There are innovations happening in dental materials all the time, and it's now getting to a point where manufacturers are bringing about more change in dentistry than dentists themselves!

But why are most dentists so resistant to change? Well, one reason is because dentistry tends to attract people to it who are quite conservative by nature. Just go to a dental convention and see how all the dentists are dressed and you get a good idea of what we are talking about!

All kidding aside, this is not to say *all* dentists are conservative, but just that the majority are, and so they don't tend to embrace change easily. This makes them typically bad business people, as change is absolutely essential to the success of a business, and it is only by embracing change, and understanding the vital role it plays in business growth, that you can truly make your practice a success.

Taking a lesson from the world of biology, Charles Darwin developed a theory of natural selection where only the strongest of a species survive. This lesson can just as easily be applied to business as it can to the natural world. For example, "survival of the fittest" should be a key mantra for any good business owner, and an even more cutting analysis would be to say that all businesses must embrace change, and ultimately either adapt or die.

So as you can see, change is important, and Michael is right to remind us that resistance to change can only ever harm a business. In dentistry, change is especially important, as the profession is changing all the time, and this process of change is getting faster with each passing year. Not only do you need to embrace the change in your business, but you also need to embrace the change in the profession. Whereas in 1993, this notion of continuous adaptation may have been about checking once a year to see that things are still working. In 2013, continuous adaptation is what's happened in the last twenty-four hours!

The Nature of Change

When we talk about change here, we are not only talking about change in the dental profession itself, but also the change that occurs in society as well. There has been a tremendous push to look and feel better, and as the baby boomer generation ages, they do not want to look or feel like they are aging. This has led to a proliferation of treatments and lifestyle changes across the social spectrum that are sold to people to make them feel younger. In fact, it's fast becoming the case that fifty is the new thirty!

These changes in society have in turn led to a number of important developments in dentistry, including porcelain veneers and short-term Orthodontic "treatments". Even in implant treatments now, people don't just want restored function—they want a solution that looks, feels and works like the teeth they lost. This has tremendously impacted the surgical approaches dentists take now, and has led to changes where we try to preserve or improve the existing site, as opposed to just working on whatever is present at the time.

Looking at this subject of dentistry as a whole, it's interesting to see that while in some areas of dentistry change has been quite dramatic, in others, there has hardly been any change at all. Amalgam fillings are one such example. There is a very limited selection of amalgam filling materials to choose from compared with composite materials that have seen at least ten different versions in the last ten years. Such has been the advance in this particular area that many of the latest products even incorporate nanotechnology!

There was a time not too long ago when as a dentist you would have to etch the tooth, dentinal prime, and then enamel bond prior to placement of the filling. Now with the latest materials, all of this can be done in a single step and there's not even any need for hot air drying. What this teaches us then is that needs-type dental work doesn't get as much innovation as want-type dentistry, as this area of the profession has a much stronger focus to change and get better.

Perhaps one of the most exciting things about dentistry today is that the pace of change gets faster every year. We're now in a world of advanced CAD CAM dentistry, where many of the leading figures in the field are carrying out procedures that would have almost been unheard of ten years ago. Who would have thought that you could actually print a 3-D model of a patient's jaw to assess and review prior to an implant surgery?

It may seem like science fiction sometimes, but such has been the advancement in technology that the profession can now help just about anyone with the resources to be able to afford it. If you're not already embracing the latest advances in the profession, then the fact of the matter is, sooner or later, you will start to fall behind.

A New Way of Thinking

In the dental profession in particular, this whole notion of change is tied up very closely in shedding the twentieth century way of thinking and moving to a much more twenty-first century type of outlook.

A major part of the problem here is that still we have a situation in dental schools where professors in their late-middle age are teaching how to do dentistry the twentieth century way. The dental schools give you the impression that as soon as you emerge from your graduation ceremony, you are sorted for life. However, this is just not the case.

To stay successful and keep on top of the latest changes and advances in the profession, you really do need to keep up with your dental education, and maintain an approach where you continue your learning throughout the course of your career.

It's shocking just how many dentists don't do this. They think they can just become an associate or buy a practice and just do the dentistry they did at dental school. Though this may seem like the easy option, just as natural selection predicts, this species is fast becoming extinct. There is a new generation of dentists emerging from universities now—a new breed of tougher, more adaptable, more "switched on" dentists who don't see university as the end of their career, but the beginning.

Please don't get the wrong impression. You might think we are knocking dental schools here, but we're really not. Most of them do a really great job providing students with a firm background in all aspects of dentistry that allow them to graduate and perform 90 percent of all procedures that they encounter upon graduation, which are typically centred around needs-oriented dentistry. Unfortunately however (and this isn't the dental schools' fault), they don't have the time or resources to educate undergraduates to a high level of competency in wants-oriented dentistry.

Also remember we earlier alluded to the fact that wants-oriented dentistry is not really embraced by most dental schools, as there is still a dichotomy over its appropriateness as being professional and ethical. Many professors would shudder at the thought of what many still perceive to be "aesthetic" cosmetic dentistry; however, the fact is dentistry has come on a long way, and the dental schools are still too caught up in the needs mentality, over the wants.

So ask yourself: Which type of dentist are you? What is your attitude to change?

To make a success of your business endeavours, you really need to embrace the fact that change will occur. If you have a low tolerance for change, then you will have to focus on being a needs-type disease-oriented dentist where not much will change in your patient base, your treatment offerings, the way you carry out your procedures, and so on.

This is not to say that being a needs-based dentist is necessarily a bad thing, but if you are to successfully grow your business, you need to accept the limiting factors that a needs-only approach will bring, and so embrace change as a constant and ever-accelerating part of your professional life.

We hope by reading Michael's thoughts on this matter you will have gained some deeper understanding of just how important change is, and how in dentistry, the change really does need to start at home! This means embracing change in your professional life, and accepting that change happens, that it's a good thing, and that it will only make you stronger as a result. Remember, stagnation is a bad thing, perhaps more in dentistry than almost any other profession.

Thankfully, there is light at the end of the tunnel, and you are holding that light now in your hands. Armed with the E-Myth philosophy, you have taken a powerful first step on the road to discovery. It's a long path, and one that starts with *you!*

The Business of Innovation

So, you've set yourself on course to embrace change in your professional life, but what next? Well now it's time to look at your business.

As we all know, sometimes we choose to enact change, but sometimes it's just thrust upon us. Unfortunately, we can't really write a guide on how to deal with every aspect of change that you encounter, but we can say this: see every change as a challenge; approach each challenge with an open mind. Whatever you do, don't let unexpected change bring you down.

This all ties in with the culture you have established for your business—a subject Michael has already spoken about a great deal. From a practical perspective, we would encourage you to adopt a culture of innovation in your business, where your team members are comfortable with change and are keen to embrace it to further the business.

Innovation in itself is a deliberate act. It can also be an intelligent act, and is a fantastic example of just how you can embrace change to help your business grow. This may be something as minor as changing the décor, or bringing in new policies as your business expands, or it may even be something far more taxing, such as hiring new team members, or creating new positions within your team such as the treatment coordinator position.

In the wider scheme of things, innovation can also include the ways in which you market yourself to the world. A practice website is pretty much a fundamental necessity in this day and age, but the way in which you utilize your website can be a means through which you can innovate, and so show potential patients just how engaged you are with dentistry, and just how driven you are to succeed.

Note that innovation is not only about new things to introduce into your business. It can also be about changing the systems in your business and changing the look and feel of your working environment—even changing the uniforms you all wear to work. In a way, the ultimate innovation may be a full office move, with a new logo, new décor, new staff, new procedures and a new focus on a different type of dentistry.

Whether this is for you, or whether it's just giving the walls a new lick of paint, it's crucial you manage change carefully with an excellent plan. With a plan, there will be less anxiety and less unknowns to confront. There will always be challenges, but the number will be less, and with a plan you always have a default position should a problem arise.

Confronting the Fear

In Michael's chapter on change, he talks a lot about the sorts of things that lead people to become fearful of change. Ask yourself, does the prospect of change frighten you, or excite you?

For many people, the fear of change is the fear of the unknown, or the fear of loss of control. If you're reading this and still find you have doubts over the nature of change, and just how you should confront it, we really do recommend you read over Michael's chapter again. What he says is quite profound in many respects as he reminds us that life is a constant flux—we are constantly moving between either an expanded or contracted state.

So, if you ever find yourself in doubt about the significance or meaning behind change in your professional and business life, remember this: change is opportunity. Without change, we would stay exactly as we are.

In the beginning, you may find it a challenge to escape the fear of change that confronts you at every turn. Though the familiar may appear safe, it is not! Only with change can you ever hope to achieve your full business potential.

Is it all starting to fit into place? We hope so. We're nearly there, but have a few more pieces of the puzzle yet to place. Now let's see what Michael has to say on the subject of time. ❧

CHAPTER
21

On the Subject
of Time

Michael E. Gerber

Take time to deliberate; but when the time for action arrives, stop thinking and go in.

—Andrew Jackson

"I'm running out of time!" dentists often lament. "I've got to learn how to manage my time more carefully!"

Of course, they see no real solution to this problem. They're just worrying the subject to death. Singing the dentist's blues.

Some make a real effort to control time. Maybe they go to time management classes, or faithfully try to record their activities during every hour of the day.

But it's hopeless. Even when dentists work harder, even when they keep precise records of their time, there's always a shortage of it. It's as if they're looking at a square clock in a round universe. Something doesn't fit. The result: the dentist is constantly chasing work, money, life.

141

And the reason is simple. Dentists don't see time for what it really is. They think of time with a small "t," rather than Time with a capital "T."

Yet Time is simply another word for *your life*. It's your ultimate asset, your gift at birth—and you can spend it any way you want. Do you know how you want to spend it? Do you have a plan?

How do *you* deal with Time? Are you even conscious of it? If you are, I bet you are constantly locked into either the future or the past. Relying on either memory or imagination.

Do you recognize these voices? "Once I get through this, I can have a drink . . . go on a vacation . . . retire." "I remember when I was young and practicing dentistry was satisfying."

As you go to bed at midnight, are you thinking about waking up at 7:00 a.m. so that you can get to the office by 8:00 a.m. so that you can go to lunch by noon, because your software people will be there at 1:30 p.m. and you've got a full schedule and a new patient scheduled for 2:30 p.m.?

Most of us are prisoners of the future or the past. While pinballing between the two, we miss the richest moments of our life—the present. Trapped forever in memory or imagination, we are strangers to the here and now. Our future is nothing more than an extension of our past, and the present is merely the background.

It's sobering to think that right now each of us is at a precise spot somewhere between the beginning of our Time (our birth) and the end of our Time (our death). No wonder everyone frets about Time. What really terrifies us is that *we're using up our life and we can't stop it.*

It feels as if we're plummeting toward the end with nothing to break our free fall. Time is out of control! Understandably, this is horrifying, mostly because the real issue is not time with a small "t" but Death with a big "D."

From the depths of our existential anxiety, we try to put Time in a different perspective—all the while pretending we can manage it. We talk about Time as though it were something other than what it is. "Time is money," we announce, as though that explains it.

But what every dentist should know is that Time is life. And Time ends! Life ends!

The big, walloping, irresolvable problem is that *we don't know how much Time we have left.*

Do you feel the fear? Do you want to get over it?

Let's look at Time more seriously.

To fully grasp Time with a capital "T," you have to ask the big Question: *How do I wish to spend the rest of my Time?*

Because I can assure you that if you don't ask that big Question with a big "Q," you will forever be assailed by the little questions. You'll shrink the whole of your life to *this time* and *next time* and the *last time*—all the while wondering, *what time is it?*

It's like running around the deck of a sinking ship worrying about where you left the keys to your cabin.

You must accept that you have only so much Time; that you're using up that Time second by precious second. And that your Time, your life, is the most valuable asset you have. Of course, you can use your Time any way you want. But unless you choose to use it as richly, as rewardingly, as excitingly, as intelligently, as *intentionally* as possible, you'll squander it and fail to appreciate it.

Indeed, if you are oblivious to the value of your Time, you'll commit the single greatest sin: You will live your life unconscious of its passing you by.

Until you deal with Time with a capital "T," you'll worry about time with a small "t" until you have no Time—or life—left. Then your Time will be history . . . along with your life.

I can anticipate the question: If Time is the problem, why not just take on fewer patients? Well, that's certainly an option, but probably not necessary. I know a dentist with a small practice who sees four times as many patients as the average, yet the doctor and staff don't work long hours. How is it possible?

This dentist has a system. By using this expert system, the employees can do everything the dentist or his associate dentists would do—everything that isn't dentist-dependent.

Be vs. Do

Remember when we all asked, "What do I want to be when I grow up?" It was one of our biggest concerns as children.

Notice that the question isn't, "What do I want to *do* when I grow up?" It's "What do I want to *be?*"

Shakespeare wrote, "To be or not to be." Not "To do or not to do."

But when you grow up, people always ask you, "What do you *do?*" How did the question change from *being* to *doing?* How did we miss the critical distinction between the two?

Even as children, we sensed the distinction. The real question we were asking was not what we would end up *doing* when we grew up, but who we would *be*.

We were talking about a *life* choice, not a *work* choice. We instinctively saw it as a matter of how we spend our Time, not what we do *in* time.

Look to children for guidance. I believe that as children we instinctively saw Time as life and tried to use it wisely. As children, we wanted to make a life choice, not a work choice. As children, we didn't know—or care—that work had to be done on time, on budget.

Until you see Time for what it really is—your life span—you will always ask the wrong question.

Until you embrace the whole of your Time and shape it accordingly, you will never be able to fully appreciate the moment.

Until you fully appreciate every second that comprises Time, you will never be sufficiently motivated to live those seconds fully.

Until you're sufficiently motivated to live those seconds fully, you will never see fit to change the way you are. You will never take the quality and sanctity of Time seriously.

And unless you take the sanctity of Time seriously, you will continue to struggle to catch up with something behind you. Your frustrations will mount as you try to snatch the second that just whisked by.

If you constantly fret about time with a small "t," then Time will blow right past you. And you'll miss the whole point, the real truth about Time: You can't manage it; you never could. You can only *live* it.

And so that leaves you with these questions: How do I live my life? How do I give significance to it? How can I be here now, in this moment?

Once you begin to ask these questions, you'll find yourself moving toward a much fuller, richer life. But if you continue to be caught up in the banal work you do every day, you're never going to find the time to take a deep breath, exhale, and be present in the now.

So, let's talk about the subject of *work*. But first, let's move on to learn what Al and Chris have to say about time. ✤

CHAPTER 22

Are You Running Out of Time?

Dr. Alan Kwong Hing
Christopher Barrow

You will never "find" time for anything. If you want time, you must make it.

—Charles Bruxton

D o you find yourself constantly running out of time? If you do, then you're not alone. Nearly all of the dentists we speak to on a regular basis complain about never having enough time to do the things they want. Sound like you? It's certainly a familiar story—one we hear time and time again.

It all starts when you leave dental school with the dream of owning your own practice. All that matters in your mind is the achievement of *owning* a practice, but rarely if ever do you consider what owning a practice really means. You'll work hard for many years to build up the capital to set up in business, but when you get there, you get caught up in a time trap that you just can't escape and have to work harder and harder just to pay the bills.

147

It's a sorry state of affairs, and one that happens all too often in dentistry. Thankfully, help is at hand. In fact, help is in your hands right now. Throughout this book Michael has spoken about the many different areas that get you caught up in this terrible time trap and now, with the help of this chapter, we hope all the other pieces will start slotting together.

Failing to Plan is Planning to Fail

As with so many things in life, failing to plan is a sure-fire way to quickly meet with failure. But it's not just planning that's the problem—it's also sticking to the plan in the first place! If, like us, you're interested in time management and decide to read more on the subject, you will find most books tell you the same thing. This is:

- Make a list
- Prioritize the list with A's as the most important, followed by B's and C's
- Do the A's first!

While it may be all well and good to make a list and prioritize the order of things to be done, it can be all too easy to get sidetracked and fail at point three. The danger here is that it can be very tempting to look at the list, see there are more straightforward B's and C's, and so occupy yourself doing these instead of doing the things that really matter. What you end up with, then, is a situation where all the A's are still there, you still have all the important work to do and you've completely tired yourself out!

As we've seen so many times throughout the course of this book, one of the main reasons dentists struggle when it comes to business is that dental schools just don't teach you about any of this! You'll do your time at school, you'll graduate and then maybe work for a few years as an associate, and then what? You'll open up your own practice and suddenly find that you need to pay the bills! Before you know it you're trying to run your business in your lunch break—or worst of all, during your precious time off—after the last patient has left your surgery.

As we hope you will appreciate by now, this is an absolute recipe for disaster, and will ultimately lead to you either making mistakes, or not performing to the best of your abilities. Your business is certain to suffer as a result. This may be because your business isn't functioning properly, or worse, may even be because your patients are given cause to complain.

Not the ideal scenario, we're sure you will agree. Thankfully though, there is a solution, and it's all tied up with Michael's excellent E-Myth philosophy.

The Art of Good Management

In previous chapters, Michael has spoken at great length about the secret to good management, and hopefully by now you will have come to realize that as a business owner, you can't do everything. Sometimes this may be because you don't have expertise in a particular area, but it may also be because quite simply, you don't have the time! That's why people are so fundamental to your business, and it's important you have systems in place that guide the people in your business in how you want your business to run.

Looking back at our list of list of points on time management, then, we realize that there is actually a fourth point that we didn't mention before: delegation. If you don't absolutely have to do something yourself, then delegate it. It really is that simple.

So our new modified list now looks like this:

- Make a list
- Prioritize the list with A's as the most important, followed by B's and C's
- Do the A's first
- Delegate everything that you don't absolutely have to do yourself

Do you have the systems and the people in place that allow you to delegate effectively? If the answer to this question is no, then we would suggest that maybe it's time you put these systems in place. And this doesn't just have to include administration tasks! Of course this will very much depend on the regulations that apply in your area; however, if you have expanded duty nurses or assistants, in some jurisdictions they can place rubber dams and can even make temporaries. If you can use expanded-duty dental hygienists/therapists, you can even have them administer local anaesthesia and place fillings. The best approach, then, is to find out what duties your team can perform in your jurisdiction and then maximize what they can do. The goal with this approach is to only do the things that you uniquely can do and delegate everything else.

Now the issue of time will come up again and again, and the only way you will get the skill set of your team to a point where you can utilize them effectively is to schedule time in the week where there are no distractions and then train them. If you have a good team, they will enjoy the ability to maximize their contribution to the practice and also to use their skills to the maximum of their abilities. This way, you can develop a team that functions at the highest levels they can.

This may sound like a simple thing to do, but you would be surprised how often we hear dentists say they only want to hire and work with smart staff, and then they do not allow them to do anything as they're too controlling and want to do everything themselves!

One of the main reasons dentists can become controlling like this is that they do not believe anyone else can do the job as well as they can. If this sounds like you, then you really do need to take a step back and look at yourself and the way you do things. You need to recognize that there are other people who can do tasks as well as you can, if not better. What you must do is set expectations and always check the result of your delegation so that everyone knows what an acceptable result is. The goal of good time management is to maximize all the things that your team can do to then free you up to do the things that uniquely only you can do. If you do this then you will be well on your way to getting the most out of your-self, and your team members. Your business will certainly flourish as a result!

Organizing Your Time

Now we've spoken a little on the art of E-Myth-style manage-ment and delegation in your dental practice, it's worthwhile spending a few moments considering how you schedule your time throughout your working week.

One of the main points to consider here is that for the vast majority of the time, you are only paid when you are working in a patient's mouth. Of course, sometimes you will be able to charge for extended diagnosis and treatment planning, but this is far and away the exception and not the rule. Generally, you will find the best time to do this kind of work is when there are no interruptions so you can focus solely on the case at hand.

To address this issue, your priority should always be to schedule time specifically for treating patients. How long you schedule is completely up to you, and depends very much on what your capacity to work is, remembering that dentistry is a very physical profession, and you need to have enough patients to treat when you are scheduled to work. The worst thing here is to be scheduled to work, but have no patients to treat! This is a major issue in dentistry, so you should impress upon your team as well as your patients why it is so important for them to show up for their allotted appointment slots.

The next issue is to schedule in time for the management and running of your practice. Even if you have a good manager in place you should still allocate time each week to review the comings and goings of the office. This may take as little as one hour, or may take as much as half a day. Either way, it must be scheduled as part of your working week and should never be cancelled or rescheduled. While you may not be directly earning money by working on the business, you will be benefiting the business in other ways that will ultimately lead to you being able to generate more income.

Do you remember in dental school how you would assign up to two hours of study for every hour of lecture? What you have to develop in your business is a similar sort of principle in which you must develop a work-in and work-on ration for your business. For example, if you work forty hours in a single week, then you allocate ten hours for work on management or leadership items. This ratio would be likely to change depending on the team you have in place and the systems you have established to keep your business running. Similarly, if you start a new project, such as an expansion of your practice, then you should increase the amount of time that will be needed each day or each week to work on your business.

Making Time for You

The final thing to consider when organising your time effectively is the time you make for yourself. Remember, what you do in your working time allows you to live the life you do. The secret, then, is to strike a balance between what you earn and how you live.

If, for example, you find that at the end of the day you have to rush out to deal with family issues, then it makes sense to schedule work on non-negotiable time early in the morning when you can devote the time needed to get things done properly. How you decide what the balance is depends on your personal relationships. It makes sense, then, to make sure your significant other understands the time commitments that are needed to own and run your own dental practice.

It's also absolutely vital that you schedule a good amount of holiday time for yourself each year. Working in dentistry is tough, we all know that, and working as a dental business owner is even tougher still. If you don't set aside time to allow yourself to recuperate, you can very quickly burn out. As we've discussed already, burnout can only be bad for your business. This is why it's essential you plan adequate holiday time for yourself.

One good way to do this is set yourself a specific time each year when you can sit down in a meeting with your family and plan holidays for the year ahead. Both of us do this each year: we pick a certain number of weeks where we want time off, and as family units, will plan what time we will have off, and what we will do in that time off. These holiday times can vary from a full week or more spent travelling abroad, to a long weekend spent closer to home.

Holiday time doesn't have to be just restful either—it can be as active and as crazy as you like. Even days spent riding bikes up mountains are a great way to unwind and let out all that stress and tension. In its own way, even a physically active mountain biking holiday is a great way to recharge your batteries.

By taking more time off, you will be better prepared, and far more productive, at work than if you spend the whole year grinding away without any holidays at all. The more productive you are, the more your income will increase as a result. When you are fresh and well rested, you can make decisions more clearly, see things in a different light.

Another important thing that a good holiday allows you to do is reconnect with your loved ones who do not see you for ten–twelve hours each day while you're working. It's a great time to rekindle the passion and take time to enjoy each other's company. After all, isn't this one of the main reasons you work in the first place?

With all these great reasons in mind a good mantra we like to use is this: to be more successful, take more holidays. We hope after reading this, you agree!

So, there you have it—our thoughts on time, in a nutshell. We hope the big picture is starting to become clear in your minds now. We're almost there, but first it's time to see what Michael has to say on the subject of work. ❦

CHAPTER 23

On the Subject of Work

Michael E. Gerber

The man who has the largest capacity for work and thought is the man who is bound to succeed.

—Henry Ford

In the business world, as the saying goes, the entrepreneur knows something about everything, the technician knows everything about something, and the switchboard operator just knows everything.

In a dental practice, dentists see their natural work as the work of the technician. The Supreme Technician. Often to the exclusion of everything else.

After all, dentists get zero preparation working as a manager and spend no time thinking as an entrepreneur—those just aren't courses offered in today's schools and colleges of dentistry. By the time they own their own dental practice, they're just doing it, doing it, doing it.

At the same time, they want everything—freedom, respect, money. Most of all, they want to rid themselves of meddling bosses and start their own practice. That way they can be their own boss and take home all the money. These dentists are in the throes of an entrepreneurial seizure.

Dentists who have been praised for their ability to treat difficult cases or their extensive knowledge of natural healthcare sciences believe they have what it takes to run a dental practice. It's not unlike the plumber who becomes a contractor because he's a great plumber. Sure, he may be a great plumber . . . but it doesn't necessarily follow that he knows how to build a practice that does this work.

It's the same for a dentist. So many of them are surprised to wake up one morning and discover that they're nowhere near as equipped for owning their own practice as they thought they were.

More than any other subject, work is the cause of obsessive-compulsive behavior by dentists.

Work. You've got to do it every single day.

Work. If you fall behind, you'll pay for it.

Work. There's either too much or not enough.

So many dentists describe work as what they do when they're busy. Some discriminate between the work they *could* be doing as dentists and the work they *should* be doing as dentists.

But according to the E-Myth, they're exactly the same thing. The work you *could* do and the work you *should* do as a dentist are identical. Let me explain.

Strategic Work vs. Tactical Work

Dentists can do only two kinds of work: strategic work and tactical work.

Tactical work is easier to understand, because it's what almost every dentist does almost every minute of every hour of every day. It's called getting the job done. It's called doing business.

Tactical work includes filing, billing, answering the telephone, going to the bank, and seeing patients.

The E-Myth says that tactical work is all the work dentists find themselves doing in a dental practice to *avoid* doing the strategic work.

"I'm too busy," most dentists will tell you.

"How come nothing goes right unless I do it myself?" they complain in frustration.

Dentists say these things when they're up to their ears in tactical work. But most dentists don't understand that if they had done more strategic work, they would have less tactical work to do.

Dentists are doing strategic work when they ask the following questions:

- Why am I a dentist?
- What will my practice look like when it's done?
- What must my practice look, act, and feel like in order for it to compete successfully?
- What are the key indicators of my practice?

Please note that I said dentists *ask* these questions when they are doing strategic work. I didn't say these are the questions they necessarily answer.

That is the fundamental difference between strategic work and tactical work. Tactical work is all about *answers*: How to do this. How to do that.

Strategic work, in contrast, is all about *questions*: What practice are we really in? Why are we in that practice? Who specifically is our practice determined to serve? When will I sell this practice? How and where will this practice be doing business when I sell it? And so forth.

Not that strategic questions don't have answers. Dentists who commonly ask strategic questions know that once they ask such a question, they're already on their way to *envisioning* the answer. Question and answer are part of a whole. You can't find the right answer until you've asked the right question.

Tactical work is much easier, because the question is always more obvious. In fact, you don't ask the tactical question; instead, the question arises from a result you need to get or a problem you need to solve. Billing a patient is tactical work. Evaluating a patient is tactical work. Firing an employee is tactical work. Performing a tooth filling is tactical work.

Tactical work is the stuff you do every day in your practice. Strategic work is the stuff you plan to do to create an exceptional practice/business/enterprise.

In tactical work, the question comes from *out there* rather than *in here*. The tactical question is about something *outside* of you, whereas the strategic question is about something *inside* of you.

The tactical question is about something you *need* to do, whereas the strategic question is about something you *want* to do. Want versus need.

If tactical work consumes you,

- you are always reacting to something outside of you;
- your practice runs you, you don't run it;
- your employees run you, you don't run them; and
- your life runs you, you don't run your life.

You must understand that the more strategic work you do, the more intentional your decisions, your practice, and your life become. *Intention* is the byword of strategic work.

Everything on the outside begins to serve you, to serve your vision, rather than forcing you to serve it. Everything you *need* to do is congruent with what you want to do. It means you have a vision, an aim, a purpose, a strategy, an *envisioned* result.

Strategic work is the work you do to *design* your practice, to design your life.

Tactical work is the work you do to *implement* the design created by strategic work.

Without strategic work, there is no design. Without strategic work, all that's left is keeping busy.

There's only one thing left to do. It's time to take action. But first, let's see what Al and Chris have to say on the subject of work. ✤

24

Work

Dr. Alan Kwong Hing
Christopher Barrow

If you love what you do, you will never do a day of work again.
—Dr. Alan Kwong Hing

We're nearly at the end now. There are only a few chapters to go, so by now we hope you have a good idea on how you might take back control of your business, and importantly, your life. Over the course of this book we've been working towards the final goal, and with the end in sight we're nearing the top of our pyramid and the end of our journey together.

One of the most important lessons we hope you have been able to glean from Michael's instructions in this book is the important distinction between working "in" your business and working "on" your business. This means to take a step back, away from the work you do every day as a dentist, and engage in work as a business owner, taking real, strategic decisions about your business, and not just about the way you do your dentistry. This can be a challenging task for

159

many people, but one you must seize with both hands if you are to make your business a real financial success.

From Tactical to Strategic

At the heart of Michael's discussion in the last chapter, he spoke about the difference between the tactical and the strategic. The tactical is what you do every day as part of your work as a dentist. This can be anything from taking x-rays to placing fillings, doing paperwork or completing a treatment plan. Essentially, anything you need to do to get the job done.

Strategic work, on the other hand, is all about the questions. It's all about taking a step back and thinking about the big picture. The trick here is not to think so much about what your business is like now, but instead look ahead to the future and think about how you'd like your practice to be. When you start to consider the differences between where you are now and where you want to be, soon enough discover the sorts of questions you should ask that will help you get to the place where you want your business to finally end up.

This whole notion is very closely tied up with the idea of strategic thinking and putting yourself in the mindset of the entrepreneur instead of the mindset of the technician. This is because working in your business won't get you, or your business, anywhere. While you're busy looking at teeth, billing patients, and so on, you're not looking at where your business will be in a few months, or even a few years' time.

If you're too wrapped up in looking at teeth, you can't be reviewing your finances and looking for signs that your business might be drifting off course. Nor can you spend your time constructing and rolling out your marketing plan. This is why you need to adopt a strategic mindset and move away from the purely tactical. The big picture is important, and it all starts with you.

Leaving the Technician Behind

One of the big difficulties with being a successful dentist is that the demands of the dental profession mean that in order to be a good dentist, you also need to be a supreme technician. That is what you were taught at dental school, and that is what gives you the feeling of accomplishment when you complete a great filling or crown preparation. Thus, it's very easy to default to what makes you feel good and what you were told makes you a successful dentist by all your professors.

The acknowledgement that you will need to focus on being an entrepreneur first and not focus on the supreme technician part of your work is the first vital step in becoming successful as a business owner. The other is to recognize that you need to invest in yourself as a dentist as the qualities you have as a technician are also vital to your business.

This means you need to embrace continuing education and working to enhance the skills that you have that make you unique as a dentist. Just as we talked about setting up a holiday schedule in our last chapter, so you should also schedule in time to attend conferences to enhance your training.

We've talked about education already throughout this book, and Michael has also provided many valuable lessons about making the most of the skill mix that's in your practice—both your own, and the skills of your team members. It is, however, worth spending a little while expanding on Michael's point about leaving the technician mentality behind.

As a dentist, chances are you got into dentistry because ultimately, you wanted to be a dentist and "do" dentistry. While there are likely many other reasons, the main reason nearly all dental practices don't work is because the person in charge is too busy "doing dentistry" and not spending enough time working on the business.

The classic mistake that nearly all principal dentists make is that they do five days of clinical work a week, sometimes more. Think about it for a moment. If you're doing clinical dentistry for five whole days a week, you're spending that entire time locked inside your surgery with the door shut. When in that time do you get a chance to have a look outside your surgery and make decisions that impact upon the way the practice actually runs?

If this is you, then we strongly recommend you take a look at your working life and think again. As Michael rightly reminds us, to be successful as a dental business owner you need to drop the technician mentality and start thinking like an entrepreneur. This means allocating some of your time to working "on" and not "in" your business.

We have spoken a great deal on the subject of time in our previous chapter, but it is worth repeating the fact that you really need to allocate time each day or each week to your business and not just to the things you need to do to get the job done. This can be an hour or two each day, to even a whole day each week, spent working on strategy and management tasks that you specifically need to take a lead on.

Take our own situation for example. Chris has a very busy schedule, and he spends a lot of his time travelling the UK and beyond meeting clients and speaking to dentists. But he only does this for four days a week. On the fifth day (usually a Monday), he allocates his time specifically working with his team, and working on the business itself. What you see, then, is that this rule doesn't just apply to dental practices, but to all sorts of business. If you don't take a step back and work on your business, your business will suffer as a result!

Seize the Moment

On the subject of work and the bigger picture, it's well worth remembering that the amount you work in any given period of time is rarely, if ever, the same. Work is hard, we all know that, but there are some times when there is far more work to do than others. This is especially true during times of opportunity, where you might find yourself in a position to take action to help your business grow. We usually call this "harvest time" as it's the time where all your good planning and careful time management go out the window and you are sometimes required to roll up your sleeves and get stuck in.

Every now and then this happens in business and it's not something you should be afraid of. Michael talked at great length in previous chapters about growth and change, and how change in itself is not a bad thing, and can in fact be a quite positive experience for your business as it allows your business to grow.

From our own experience, we are both prepared to sacrifice our short-term strategic work in favour of a more tactical approach to get things done. The reason we can do this is because we already have the systems that Michael talks about in place to cover our period where we don't have to be personally steering every single decision. Everyone in each of our teams knows what their role is and what's expected of them, and in most cases, we don't need to take a lead as the day-to-day part of the business is now a well-oiled machine.

Quite simply, we have the systems, the flexibility, and the mindset to rise to the latest challenge that has presented itself.

Applying this thinking now to your practice in particular, ask yourself: Do you have these three key features in place? What's your attitude to change and to growth? How would you cope with an unexpected development, such as a key member of staff leaving, or the purchase of a new piece of equipment?

Only with the right approach to the subject of work and your duel role both as a tactician and a strategist—as a dentist and as a business owner—will you be able to make your practice a viable, long-term success.

We're almost there now. Are you ready for the final piece? Let's see what Michael has to say about taking action. ✤

On the Subject of Taking Action

Michael E. Gerber

Deliberation is the work of many men. Action, of one alone.
—Charles de Gaulle

I t's time to get started, time to take action. Time to stop thinking about the old practice and start thinking about the new practice. It's not a matter of coming up with better practices; it's about reinventing the practice of dentistry.

And the dentist has to take personal responsibility for it.

That's you.

So sit up and pay attention!

You, the dentist, have to be interested. You cannot abdicate accountability for the practice of dentistry, the administration of dentistry, or the finance of dentistry.

Although the goal is to create systems into which dentists can plug reasonably competent people—systems that allow the practice to run without them—dentists must take responsibility for that happening.

I can hear the chorus now: "But we're dentists! We shouldn't have to know about this." To that I say: whatever. If you don't give a flip about your practice, fine—close your mind to new knowledge and accountability. But if you want to succeed, then you'd better step up and take responsibility, and you'd better do it now.

All too often, dentists take no responsibility for the business of dentistry but instead delegate tasks without any understanding of what it takes to do them; without any interest in what their people are actually doing; without any sense of what it feels like to be at the front desk when a patient comes in and has to wait for forty-five minutes; and without any appreciation for the entity that is creating their livelihood.

Dentists can open the portals of change in an instant. All you have to do is say, "I don't want to do it that way anymore." Saying it will begin to set you free—even though you don't yet understand what the practice will look like after it's been reinvented.

This demands an intentional leap from the known into the unknown. It further demands that you live there—in the unknown— for a while. It means discarding the past, everything you once believed to be true.

Think of it as soaring rather than plunging.

Thought Control

You should now be clear about the need to organize your thoughts first, and then your business. Because the organization of your thoughts is the foundation for the organization of your business.

If we try to organize our business without organizing our thoughts, we will fail to attack the problem.

We have seen that organization is not simply time management. Nor is it people management. Nor is it tidying up desks or alphabetizing patient files. Organization is first, last, and always cleaning up the mess of our minds.

By learning how to *think* about the practice of dentistry, by learning how to *think* about your priorities, and by learning how to *think* about your life, you'll prepare yourself to do righteous battle with the forces of failure.

Right thinking leads to right action—and now is the time to take action. Because it is only through action that you can translate thoughts into movement in the real world, and, in the process, find fulfillment.

So, first *think* about what you want to do. Then *do* it. Only in this way will you be fulfilled.

How do you put the principles we've discussed in this book to work in your dental practice? To find out, accompany me down the path once more:

1. *Create a story about your practice.* Your story should be an idealized version of your dental practice, a vision of what the preeminent dentist in your field should be and why. Your story must become the very heart of your practice. It must become the spirit that mobilizes it, as well as everyone who walks through the doors. Without this story, your practice will be reduced to plain work.

2. *Organize your practice so that it breathes life into your story.* Unless your practice can faithfully replicate your story in action, it all becomes fiction. In that case, you'd be better off not telling your story at all. And without a story, you'd be better off leaving your practice the way it is and just hoping for the best.

Here are some tips for organizing your dental practice:

- Identify the key functions of your practice.
- Identify the essential processes that link those functions.
- Identify the results you have determined your practice will produce.
- Clearly state in writing how each phase will work.

Take it step by step. Think of your practice as a program, a piece of software, a system. It is a collaboration, a collection of processes dynamically interacting with one another.

Of course, your practice is also people.

3. *Engage your people in the process.* Why is this the third step rather than the first? Because, contrary to the advice most business experts will give you, you must never engage your people in the process until you yourself are clear about what you intend to do.

The need for consensus is a disease of today's addled mind. It's a product of our troubled and confused times. When people don't know what to believe in, they often ask others to tell them. To ask is not to lead but to follow.

The prerequisite of sound leadership is first to know where you wish to go.

And so, "What do I want?" becomes the first question; not, "What do they want?" In your own practice, the vision must first be yours. To follow another's vision is to abdicate your personal accountability, your leadership role, your true power.

In short, the role of leader cannot be delegated or shared. And without leadership, no dental practice will ever succeed.

Despite what you have been told, win-win is a secondary step, not a primary one. The opposite of win-win is not necessarily they lose.

Let's say "they" can win by choosing a good horse. The best choice will not be made by consensus. "Guys, what horse do you think we should ride?" will always lead to endless and worthless discussions. By the time you're done jawing, the horse will have already left the post.

Before you talk to your people about what you intend to do in your practice and why you intend to do it, you need to reach agreement with yourself.

It's important to know (1) exactly what you want, (2) how you intend to proceed, (3) what's important to you and what isn't, and (4) what you want the practice to be and how you want it to get there.

Once you have that agreement, it's critical that you engage your people in a discussion about what you intend to do and why. Be clear—both with yourself and with them.

The Story

The story is paramount because it is your vision. Tell it with passion and conviction. Tell it with precision. Never hurry a great story. Unveil it slowly. Don't mumble or show embarrassment. Never apologize or display false modesty. Look your audience in the eyes and tell your story as though it is the most important one they'll ever hear about business. Your business. The business into which you intend to pour your heart, your soul, your intelligence, your imagination, your time, your money, and your sweaty persistence.

Get into the storytelling zone. Behave as though it means everything to you. Show no equivocation when telling your story.

These tips are important because you're going to tell your story over and over—to patients, to new and old employees, to dentists, to associate dentists, and to your family and friends. You're going to tell it at your church or synagogue, to your card-playing or fishing buddies, and to organizations such as Kiwanis, Rotary, YMCA, Hadassah, and Boy Scouts.

There are few moments in your life when telling a great story about a great business is inappropriate.

If it is to be persuasive, you must love your story. Do you think Walt Disney loved his Disneyland story? Or Ray Kroc his McDonald's story? What about Dave Smith at Federal Express? Or Debbie Fields at Mrs. Field's Cookies? Or Tom Watson Jr. at IBM?

Do you think these people loved their stories? Do you think others loved (and *still* love) to hear them? I daresay *all* successful entrepreneurs have loved the story of their business. Because that's what true entrepreneurs do. They tell stories that come to life in the form of their business.

Remember: A great story never fails. A great story is always a joy to hear.

In summary, you first need to clarify, both for yourself and for your people, the *story* of your practice. Then you need to detail the *process* your practice must go through to make your story become reality.

I call this the business development process. Others call it reengineering, continuous improvement, reinventing your practice, or total quality management.

Whatever you call it, you must take three distinct steps to succeed:

- *Innovation.* Continue to find better ways of doing what you do.
- *Quantification.* Once that is achieved, quantify the impact of these improvements on your practice.
- *Orchestration.* Once these improvements are verified, orchestrate this better way of running your practice so that it becomes your standard, to be repeated time and again.

In this way, the system works—no matter who's using it. And you've built a practice that works consistently, predictably, systematically. A practice you can depend on to operate exactly as promised, every single time.

Your vision, your people, your process—all linked.

A superior dental practice is a creation of your imagination, a product of your mind. So fire it up and get started! Now let's see what Al and Chris have to say about taking action. ❧

CHAPTER 26

Taking Action

Dr. Alan Kwong Hing
Christopher Barrow

Go confidently in the direction of your dreams. Live the life you have imagined.

—Henry David Thoreau

Congratulations! You've reached the end of what we hope has been a rewarding and eye-opening journey through the world of *The E-Myth Dentist*. If you're anything like either of us when we first read Michael Gerber's E-Myth philosophy, your head will be buzzing with ideas, and you will hardly know where to start! Exciting, isn't it?

By now, we hope some of the wisdom instilled through this book will have started to set a few gears in motion, and you've realized that if you want to turn your business life around, there's a lot of work that needs to be done first.

But don't kid yourself—the journey is not an easy one, and one of the hardest parts is taking that first tentative step. After all, intention without action is merely a delusion, so don't be fooled: this journey is going to be *hard*. Perhaps the hardest part is letting go of your old, technician way of thinking, but when you do, we can honestly say that your whole life will change for the better.

Of course, we are not saying that we have all the answers, but with our practical experience as a business coach and a dentist who owns multiple offices, we have a wealth of experience that we have shared with you. Some of this is to help you understand that we know your pain and problems, and that we have successfully worked through these trials in real life situations.

Throughout our working lives, we have had many different occasions where we have incorporated Michael's teachings—and we have not been disappointed.

Strangely enough, at the time of writing this book, we've just come across a dentist who is the perfect E-Myth case. This dentist owns five practices spread out across a large area of the country. The business is financially successful, but behind the scenes, it's falling apart. This is because the owner is a micro-manager, and the business is literally consuming his life. He has made himself the manager of finance, marketing, lead generation, lead conversion, HR, and even operations. The owner is, in effect, in charge of everything.

Ok, so the business is making money at the moment, but the whole thing is consuming him! And it's bad for the business, too. The company is at a point now where a patient newsletter from six months ago still hasn't been sent out, as the business owner wasn't happy with how it was written and so decided he was going to do it himself. That's a six-month delay . . . on a newsletter. Now multiply that by 10,000 other tasks and you see the problem!

Does this sound like you? Are you too caught up in managing everything that your business is suffering? Or perhaps you're at the other end of the spectrum and are so consumed by "doing dentistry" that you have absolutely no idea what's going on in your business?

Hopefully, after reading this book, you will have some idea what needs to be done. Well here it is, the final act—it's time to take some action!

Where Do I Start?

One of the worst things that can happen to you at this point is to fall at the first hurdle. So you've got the ideas, and you know what you want to achieve, but you struggle to get things moving. For many people, one of the biggest challenges is just knowing where to start!

Don't worry—we've all been at the same point at some time in our lives. The first thing that we need to remind you, then, is that it's not where do *I* start, but where do *we* start.

This has been the whole point of everything Michael has talked about through this book. People are important. Recognize the skills your team members have at their disposal and put them to use. Don't do things alone, and be prepared to trust! Share with your team what you want to do with the business to make it more successful. They will then be more active in supporting your plans, and in many cases will be the ones who actually make it happen!

So . . . where to begin? If we continue with our example for a moment, the first thing that he needs to do is sit down and sort out a list of things that need to be done. This massive to-do list needs to be spread out over ninety days, six months, or maybe even a year. This list needs to be prioritized and time-activated. Tasks then need to be assigned to the individual responsible for it, and best suited to deliver it.

The object of this exercise is to leave the owner with very little to do; after all, with the right *systems* in place, the owner shouldn't have to do all that much. Our dentist needs to decide how many days he wants to be a dentist and "do dentistry." He then needs to assign himself with time for management of his business—ideally no more than a day per week.

This can be a difficult mindset to take on, as you are so used to working as an hourly-billing and paid dentist that taking time off from "doing dentistry" can feel like you are losing income. Trust us when we say that time and time again, when you tighten up your schedule, you will be able to deliver the same amount of dentistry in 20 percent less time. In fact, in many cases, you can actually bill more in a shorter amount of time, as you are more focused and more efficient.

Quite naturally, this can be something of a shock to the system. If you're not used to giving up control, then you're going to need to do some serious soul searching. Remember, you're the *business owner*. There's a reason you employ staff, and that reason is so that they can work for you and help your business grow!

Embrace the fact that your dental practice is a business and stop making excuses. After all the schooling and costs you have undertaken, you owe it to yourself, and everyone who has supported you along the way, to make it work and pay for all your efforts.

Letting Go

In our experience, there are two distinct elements to "Taking Action." On the one side, we have the performance element. That is, structuring a coherent plan that encompasses your vision, and putting the systems in place to help you achieve your goal.

On the other side we have the emotional part of the equation. This is by far and away the harder of the two elements, and is something you need to both recognize, and come to terms with, if you are to make your business a success.

Quite simply, you need to overcome the emotional barrier that's keeping you tied down as a technician within your own business.

This may sound simple, but experience tells us that it's not. If it was such a simple task, then why isn't every dental practice around the world a success? Why would we need business books at all? When it comes to the emotion of dropping the technician mentality, we are sure that letting go is probably as much as ten times harder than the performance side.

Of course, for some people this whole concept is far easier than others. Some people may well struggle with giving up the technician mentality and adopting the mantle of leadership, but for others it may be far simpler. Whichever camp you fall into, if there's one piece of advice we can leave you with it's this: don't wait.

There is no such thing as the right or wrong time to embrace E-Myth. The only thing you can be sure of is that the longer you leave it, the longer your life will be consumed by your business, and the longer your business will struggle.

Let us put it this way: if everyone had to wait for the right time to open a business, then no businesses would have opened. The opportunity for you is out there, it's waiting, it's calling you. With your copy of *The E-Myth Dentist* in hand, a life-changing experience is just around the corner. E-Myth changed both of our lives, and we know it can change yours, too.✤

AFTERWORD

Michael E. Gerber

For more than three decades, I've applied the E-Myth principles I've shared with you here to the successful development of thousands of small businesses throughout the world. Many have been dental practices—from small companies to large corporations, with dentists specializing in every field from wellness care to straight dentistry.

Few rewards are greater than seeing these E-Myth principles improve the work and lives of so many people. Those rewards include seeing these changes:

- Lack of clarity—clarified.
- Lack of organization—organized.
- Lack of direction—shaped into a path that is clearly, lovingly, passionately pursued.
- Lack of money or money poorly managed—money understood instead of coveted; created instead of chased; wisely spent or invested instead of squandered.
- Lack of committed people—transformed into a cohesive community working in harmony toward a common goal; discovering one another and themselves in the process; all the while expanding their understanding, their know-how, their interest, their attention.

After working with so many dentists, I know that a practice can be much more than what most become. I also know that nothing is preventing you from making your practice all that it can be. It takes only desire and the perseverance to see it through.

In this book—the next of its kind in the E-Myth Expert series— the E-Myth principles have been complemented and enriched by stories from real-life dentists and business entrepreneurs, such as Dr. Alan Kwong Hing and Christopher Barrow, who have put these principles to use in their practice. These dentists have had the desire and perseverance to achieve success beyond their wildest dreams. Now you, too, can join their ranks.

I hope this book has helped you clear your vision and set your sights on a very bright future.

To your practice and your life, good growing!

ABOUT THE AUTHOR

Michael E. Gerber

Michael E. Gerber is the international legend, author, and thought leader behind the E-Myth series of books, including *The E-Myth Revisited, E-Myth Mastery, The E-Myth Manager, The E-Myth Enterprise, The Most Successful Small Business in the World and Awakening the Entrepreneur Within.* Collectively, Mr. Gerber's books have sold millions of copies worldwide. Michael Gerber is the founder of Michael E. Gerber Companies, E-Myth Worldwide, The Dreaming Room™, and his newest venture, Design, Build, Launch & Grow™. Since 1977, Mr. Gerber's companies have served the business development needs of over 70,000 business clients in over 145 countries. Regarded by his avid followers as the thought leader of entrepreneurship worldwide, Mr. Gerber has been called by Inc. Magazine, "the world's #1 small business guru." A highly sought-after speaker and strategist, who has single handedly been accountable for the transformation of small business worldwide, Michael lives with his wife, Luz Delia, in Carlsbad, California.

ABOUT THE CO-AUTHORS

Dr. Alan Kwong Hing

Dr. Alan Kwong Hing graduated with his Doctor of Dental Surgery degree (with distinction) from the University of Western Ontario in London, Ontario, Canada. He received the University Gold Medal and completed a concurrent Master's Degree in Pathology. In 1989, Alan represented Canada at the International Association for Dental Research competition in Dublin, Ireland. He won the prestigious Hatton Award for his predoctoral research with MRI's.

Alan is the founder of the Maritime Dental Group which owns dental practices in Canada and Scotland. He has been a partner in several dental corporate groups in Canada and the US.

He is a practicing dentist and is passionate about providing patients with dental implant based treatment solutions. He lectures internationally with a focus on incorporating dental implants into a general dental practice, dental practice management and team building. He offers live practical coaching on many aspects of the dental world.

Alan has a strong understanding of the dental market and how to grow dental practices, whilst ensuring incentives and drivers work for both dentists and auxiliary staff.

He has significant experience in recruiting and managing associate dentists and support staff, as well as establishing relationships with suppliers.

His mantra is, "Throw out the book and let's invent this thing as if we have no boundaries."

ABOUT THE CO-AUTHORS

Christopher Barrow

Chris Barrow has been active as a trainer, consultant, coach and mentor to the UK and Irish dental profession for over 20 years.

Naturally direct, assertive and determined, he has the ability to reach conclusions quickly, as well as the sharp reflexes and lightness of touch to innovate, change tack and push boundaries. As a speaker he is dynamic, energetic and charismatic.

Chris spent the first 17 years of his career in the corporate sector and followed this with 26 years of self-employment. The different dynamics of both worlds have given him the valuable gift of knowing how to operate – and communicate – in both.

In 1987 Chris was active in the establishment of the Institute for Financial Planning, a UK organization representing the first fee-based Financial Planners; Chris specialized in working with small businesses.

In 1993 Chris decided to make the transition into business coaching and became one of the first UK students at Coach University, from where he graduated as a certified coach. Recognizing the opportunity in the dental profession, 1997 saw the creation of The Dental Business School (DBS) and the development of a twelve-month business coaching program for dental practice owners and their teams, delivered to over 700 UK dental practices in the following ten years.

Chris now acts as an occasional Non-Executive Director for dental corporations and retailers.

His main focus is as a founding partner in 7connections, a privately-owned company that specializes in training, consulting, coaching, and mentoring in independent dentistry across the European Union and which also takes minority equity positions in private practices.

ABOUT THE SERIES

The E-Myth Expert series brings Michael E. Gerber's proven E-Myth philosophy to a wide variety of different professional business areas. The E-Myth, short for "Entrepreneurial Myth," is simple: Too many small businesses fail to grow because their leaders think like technicians, not entrepreneurs. Gerber's approach gives small enterprise leaders practical, proven methods that have already helped transform tens of thousands of businesses. Let the E-Myth Expert series boost your professional business today!

Books in the series include:
The E-Myth Attorney
The E-Myth Accountant
The E-Myth Optometrist
The E-Myth Chiropractor
The E-Myth Financial Advisor
The E-Myth Landscape Contractor
The E-Myth Architect
The E-Myth Real Estate Brokerage
The E-Myth Insurance Store
The E-Myth Real Estate Investor
The E-Myth Dentist

Forthcoming books in the series include:
The E-Myth Nutritionist
The E-Myth Bookkeeper
. . . and 300 more industries and professions

Learn more at: www.michaelegerber.com/co-author

Have you created an E-Myth enterprise? Would you like to become a co-author of an E-Myth book in your industry? Go to www.michaelegerber.com/co-author.

186

THE MICHAEL E. GERBER
ENTREPRENEUR'S LIBRARY
It Keeps Growing . . .

Thank you for reading another E-Myth Vertical book.

Who do you know who is an expert in their industry?

Who has applied the E-Myth to the improvement of their practice as Dr. Alan Kwong Hing and Christopher Barrow have?

Who can add immense value to others in his or her industry by sharing what he or she has learned?

Please share this book with that individual and share that individual with us.

We at Michael E. Gerber Companies are determined to transform the state of small business and entrepreneurship worldwide. *You can help.*

To find out more, email us at Michael E. Gerber Partners, at gerber@michaelegerber.com.

To find out how YOU can apply the E-Myth to YOUR practice, contact us at gerber@michaelegerber.com.

Thank you for living your Dream, and changing the world.

Authors of Business Design

Michael E. Gerber, Co-Founder/Chairman
Michael E. Gerber Companies™
Creator of The E-Myth Evolution™
P.O. Box 131195, Carlsbad, CA 92013
760-752-1812 O • 760-752-9926 F
gerber@michaelegerber.com
www.michaelegerber.com

Join The Evolution^{SM}

Attend the Dreaming Room™ Trainings
www.michaelegerber.com/dreaming-room

Awaken the Entrepreneur Within You
www.michaelegerber.com/facilitator-training

Michael E. Gerber Partners
www.michaelegerber.com/are-you-the-one

Listen to the Michael E. Gerber Radio Show
www.blogtalkradio.com/michaelegerber

Watch the latest videos
www.youtube.com/michaelegerber

Connect on LinkedIn
www.linkedin.com/in/michaelegerber

Connect on Facebook
www.facebook.com/MichaelEGerberCo

CPSIA information can be obtained
at www.ICGtesting.com
Printed in the USA
BVOW08*1519021216

469627BV00006B/24/P

9 781618 350251